Beggars, Cheats
and Forgers

Beggars, Cheats and Forgers

A history of frauds through the ages

David Thomas

PEN & SWORD
HISTORY

First published in Great Britain in 2014 by
PEN & SWORD HISTORY
An imprint of
Pen & Sword Books Ltd
47 Church Street
Barnsley
South Yorkshire
S70 2AS

ISBN 978-1-78159-327-1

Typeset by Concept, Huddersfield, West Yorkshire, HD4 5JL.
Printed and bound in England by CPI Group (UK) Ltd, Croydon CR0 4YY.

Pen & Sword Books Ltd incorporates the imprints of Pen & Sword Archaeology,
Atlas, Aviation, Battleground, Discovery, Family History, History, Maritime,
Military, Naval, Politics, Railways, Select, Social History, Transport, True Crime,
and Claymore Press, Frontline Books, Leo Cooper, Praetorian Press,
Remember When, Seaforth Publishing and Wharncliffe.

For a complete list of Pen & Sword titles please contact
PEN & SWORD BOOKS LIMITED
47 Church Street, Barnsley, South Yorkshire, S70 2AS, England
E-mail: enquiries@pen-and-sword.co.uk
Website: www.pen-and-sword.co.uk

Contents

List of Illustrations

Thomas Harman, *Caveat for Common Cursitors* (1567).

Nicholas Jennings, the notorious Elizabethan beggar, who lived as a gentleman while not begging. Jennings is shown in both his suits of clothes from *Groundwork of Cony-Catching* (1592).

Jennings in the pillory, dressed as both a gentleman and a beggar, from Harman, *Caveat for Common Cursitors* (1566).

Joe Johnson, the famed black beggar, who walked round London with a ship on his head in the 1870s.

Richard Watts founded a charity in Rochester, which provided a night's accommodation plus meals and four pence, to six poor travellers who were neither rogues nor travellers.

The interior of a room in Watts's charity in Rochester.

Acknowledgements

I should like to thank Simon Fowler for much valuable advice and Andrea Thomas and Amanda Spencer for commenting on the text, Hope Thomas for photography and Philip Hall for map making.

Introduction

The internet has changed nothing. Despite the widespread belief that it has opened up a whole new realm of criminal activity, there is nothing new about the ways in which people extort money from others by cheating. People who commit financial frauds, forge documents, pretend to be disabled, hungry or in prison are the same in the modern era as they were in the past.

However, by looking at a range of dishonest activities, we can learn a lot about the psychology of the criminals and their victims and how the most talented villains have learned to prey on their victims' greed, credulity and kindness. The essence of a great beggar, a successful begging letter writer, a leading con man or a forger is to get a deep understanding of their potential victims – what motivates them and how to exploit their human weaknesses for profit. As we will discover, there is little difference between a sixteenth century cheat and modern cyber criminals whose 'spear fishing' and 'watering holes' are merely fancy names for techniques which have been in use for hundreds of years.

In the end, if we live long enough, it is likely that we will all fall victim to some sort of scam. The best thing we can do is to hope to postpone the event and minimize the damage. By learning about the behaviours of the cheats, we are giving ourselves a fighting chance of escaping from their clutches.

This book describes the careers of some of the greatest practitioners of these dark arts: Mark Hofmann from Salt Lake City, surely the world's greatest forger; Bernie Madoff who, until the roof fell in, was the most successful con man ever; as well as a supporting cast of dozens of other rogues, sturdy beggars, forgers and con artists. It covers both real cheats and their fictional equivalents. Sometimes it is hard to tell the difference. Bampfylde Moore Carew was the eighteenth century King of the Beggars and his *Life and Adventures* was a best-seller for nearly 100 years, but, although we know that he really existed, it is hard to tell how much of his *Life* was an invention and how much was real.

George Atkins Brine was Carew's nineteenth century equivalent and he made a shrewd remark about his chosen lifestyle: 'Imposture like every other trade, requires for thorough success a long apprenticeship and a keen observance of the foibles and weaknesses of human nature'. As Brine said, a successful impostor requires a good knowledge of psychology and by studying the practices of cheats and the reactions of their victims, we can learn a lot about our own nature. So this is really a book about ourselves.

The twentieth century successor of Carew and Brine was W.H. Davies and he is of great interest, because for him the life of a beggar was a lifestyle choice. Davies did not choose the marginal existence of a hobo because he was down on his luck. Instead it was a conscious decision, motivated by his love for the pleasure and freedom of the road; being able to get up when he chose and go where he wished.

As we will discover, the way people cheat each other does not change over time. The motives and methods of people who produced forgeries of Shakespearean documents in the nineteenth century were similar to those of Mark Hofmann, the Mormon forger, or the creator of false records about the death of Heinrich Himmler. Bernie Madoff's techniques were little different from those of the villains Dickens described in *Martin Chuzzlewit* and *Little Dorrit*. Most modern scams on the internet employ the same approach as their nineteenth century predecessors. Have you been the subject of a highly-personalized email or telephone call designed to extract financial information from you, or have you been asked to give money to a charity you have never heard of, or been promised a fortune from Nigeria? If so, your experience is no different from any of the hundreds of victims of the Spanish Prisoner scam of the 1890s.

People read and write about crime partly because it is an endlessly fascinating subject and partly because we all enjoy the slight sense of fear and outrage that a good crime story gives us. However, it is clear that different types of crime were of particular concern to readers at different times and we now have a tool that enables us to discover more about this. Google's Ngram tracks the usage over time of particular words or phrases in the millions of books they have scanned. In the period from 1800 to 2000, the most popular crime for readers was murder and this is mentioned about twice as many times as the second most popular crime: fraud. Thieves, burglars and forgers pretty much track each other in popularity over the same period. But go back another 200 years and people were much more bothered about beggars than murderers. Gradually, people's concerns shifted until by 1800 murder was well ahead of begging in the fears of the reading public.

Of the words used to describe people who lived itinerant lives, the word 'tramp' came into prominence during the nineteenth century. From a low base in 1800, it was mentioned in increasing numbers of books until it reached a peak between 1890 and 1920 when it declined. The word 'vagrant' was less popular, being used about a quarter of the number of times as 'tramp'. Apart from the early seventeenth century, the high point of interest in beggars was in the decade from 1800 to 1810 and it is used pretty steadily thereafter until 1900, when its use began to fall away. The use of the word 'homeless' came into prominence in the early 1980s, while the currently fashionable phrase 'rough sleepers' is hardly referred to before the year 2000.

The reason why begging was of such concern in the early seventeenth century was the growing popularity of rogue literature. This began in the sixteenth century, when Thomas Harman, a Kentish gentleman, interrogated the beggars travelling past his house along Watling Street and recorded his findings. The tradition continued through the seventeenth century and in the eighteenth century we begin to see the first biographies of beggars. By the nineteenth century we have the great social observers, notably Henry Mayhew, as well as Charles Dickens, who wrote on many aspects of rogue life, including thieves, sturdy beggars and begging letter writers.

Rogue literature was written as a form of entertainment 'to shorten the lives of long winter nights', but it also provided its readers with insights into the operation of crime, begging, fraud and villainy. It was designed to warn people about the risks to which they were exposed from cheats and rogues of all sorts, but also to give them a frisson of nervousness by telling some scary but plausible tales. It is hoped that the present work will do the same.

David Thomas,
October 2013

Chapter One

The Greatest Con Men

*If it looks like a duck, if it waddles like a duck
and if it quacks like a duck, it must be a duck*

All the characters described in this book – sturdy beggars, promoters of postal scams, forgers and con men – used dishonest methods to obtain money. The great con men are, in some senses, the kings of the cheats. Those described here all obtained huge sums of money as a result of their dishonesty and one, Bernie Madoff, probably stole more than anyone else in history. However, the scale of their activities is the one thing that does make these men stand out in our rogues' gallery. In other ways, as we shall discover, they used very similar psychological techniques to other cheats, luring their victims into a web of deceit and lies in order to get hold of their money. Sometimes, however, these con men found themselves caught in the web of their own deceptions.

We will be looking at the criminal careers of some of the greatest con men of the past 200 years: John Sadleir the Irish banker; William '520 per cent' Miller, who was the role model for Charles Ponzi of the eponymous scheme; Bernie Madoff, who took Ponzi's scheme to greater heights than was ever thought possible; and Sir Allen Stanford, the Texan cricket fan and cheat. In addition we will be considering two fictional Dickensian characters – Mr Merdle from *Little Dorrit* and Tigg Montague (also known as Montague Tigg) from *Martin Chuzzlewit*.

Why mix fiction with fact? Well, there are two reasons: first, both Dickens's villains are based on reality; Merdle is partly modelled on Sadleir, while Montague is sometimes claimed to be the first identifiable creator of a Ponzi scheme. The second reason is that Dickens saw further into the human heart, including the hearts of confidence tricksters than a whole faculty of criminologists, sociologists and journalists.

The most useful analysis of financial fraud in recent years was published by the Florida-based Venezuelan financial analyst, Alex Dalmady. He said that the simplest way to recognize a fraud was the duck theory – if it quacks like a duck and walks like a duck and has a bill like a duck, then it is a duck. Financial ducks do not have bills or quacks or funny walks, but they do have similar characteristics by which it is possible to recognize them.

Of course, for one thing they are all too good to be true. Some are very obviously much too good to be true; Gumi, a financial pyramid scheme operating in Bolivia during the mid-1990s offered to pay 20 per cent a month. The cleverest and most subtle financial ducks, such as Madoff and Stanford, only pay returns slightly above what is reasonable and so can survive for years because their activities are not easy to recognize as scams. And they do something that nobody else can. It was rumoured that Gumi offered such good returns because it was financing drug lords, but why would such men need to borrow at such high rates? Their real problem is how to safely launder the millions they generate.

In addition, frauds have very few people providing appropriate governance. Madoff's giant empire was audited by a single accountant, who operated out of a small office in upstate New York. Finally, there are few incentives for whistle blowers. As the author Diana Henriques pointed out, Ponzi schemes are crimes where, until the last minute, there are no victims. The existing investors are happy receiving interest funded by new investors and they have no reason to rock the boat – until the boat sinks. As we will see, in many cases the authorities became suspicious of these con men but were unable to find any investors who were willing to say anything bad about them. The victims of Miller, Ponzi and the others were gaining their crazy rates of interest and were quite happy until the day the music stopped.

When I first began thinking about this chapter, I took the view that these men were simply evil; as we will see, Ponzi was happy to steal his wife's endowment and Madoff stole indiscriminately from friends and family. However, the reality is more complex than that and, while what they all did was certainly unforgivable and evil, their reasons for doing it were more subtle.

All the crimes we are considering are more or less versions of the Ponzi scheme. This phrase has become much better known since the Madoff crime, but it has been around in the USA since 1920. Such schemes are fraudulent investments which pay returns to their investors from their own money or from subsequent investors, rather than from profits earned from real assets such as stocks and shares. Typically, investors are offered high rates of return by a fraudster. The money they invest is not invested in any assets and the fraudster relies on attracting money from new investors to enable the payment of future dividends.

Because the returns on offer are so good, investors often leave their capital and dividends invested with the scheme and so Ponzi schemes can last for years – Madoff managed to keep his going for at least 16 years. Eventually the schemes collapse, either because the proprietor runs off, or the fraud is exposed or because some external factor leads investors to try to withdraw their money and it rapidly becomes apparent that there is no cash left for them to withdraw.

Madoff and Stanford were both exposed because the financial crisis of 2008 made the cracks in their schemes visible.

Charles Ponzi's scheme came to him after a failed attempt to set up a business-listing publication, a bit like Yellow Pages. The business failed, but a Spanish company had sent him a letter requesting information and enclosed an international reply coupon (IRC). The purpose of international postal reply coupons is to allow someone in one country to send a coupon to a correspondent in another country, who could use it to pay the postage of a reply. IRCs were priced at the cost of postage in the country of purchase, but could be exchanged for stamps to cover the cost of postage in the country where redeemed; if these values were different, there was a potential profit.

Inflation after the First World War had greatly decreased the cost of postage in Spain and Italy expressed in US dollars, so that a coupon could be bought cheaply in Spain or Italy and exchanged for US stamps of higher value, which could then be cashed in. Charles Ponzi could exchange 1 US dollar for 20 Italian lira. With 20 lira he could buy 66 coupons that he could exchange for 66 US stamps worth $3.30, a gross profit of 230 per cent. The essential idea behind Ponzi's scheme was legitimate – making a profit because of variations in rates of exchange is a normal commercial activity and is referred to as arbitrage. However, as we will discover, Ponzi's particular version of arbitrage was fraudulent in the extreme.

One thing many of our con men had in common, was that they were outsiders looking in on a world they were anxious to join. Tigg Montague was the ultimate outsider – we first meet him trying to scrounge money to pay his bill at the local inn. He was 'very dirty and very jaunty; very bold and very mean; very swaggering and very slinking; very much like a man who might have been something better and unspeakably like a man who deserved to be something worse'.

Sadleir was also an outsider – an Irish Catholic who tried to straddle the worlds of Irish politics and the English establishment. He served as MP for Carlow and was a founder of the Catholic Defence Association, but he also accepted a junior ministerial post in the government of Lord Aberdeen, which caused huge offence to his fellow Irish MPs and led to the loss of his seat in Parliament at Westminster. According to his biographer, Sadleir was socially awkward; and so when Dickens produced a fictionalized version of him in *Little Dorrit*, he described him as an important figure in society, but a man who was slightly ill at ease. Dickens describes how 'Mr Merdle stopped and looked at the table cloth as he usually did when he found himself observed or listened to'.

Charles Ponzi was born Carlo Pietro Giovanni Guglielmo Tebaldo Ponzi in Lugo, Italy, in 1882. Much of his early life is hard to discover because he usually told lies about himself. He claimed that he went to university in Rome, but that he spent his time there on pleasurable activities, not study. When he arrived in the United States in 1903, he claimed to have only had $2.50 in cash because he had become the victim of a cardsharp on the boat. He later said that he landed in the USA with $2.50 in cash and a million dollars in dreams. However, Ponzi's overwhelming characteristic, like most con men, was supreme self-confidence. Towards the end of his short-lived career, there was a run on his business with people queuing to withdraw their money. Ponzi did not panic; instead, he paid out two million dollars and provided coffee and doughnuts to those in the queue. Some people were taken in and continued to leave their money in his hands.

Madoff's father was an unsuccessful businessman; his first venture was making punch bags and other sporting goods based on the Joe Palooka comic strip character. In 1951 his business went down owing $90,000 and, having failed in another venture, he eventually became a 'finder', raising investments in companies in return for a fee.

Sir Allen Stanford seems to have made himself into an outsider; although he was a Texan, he adopted English interests and took up English pursuits. He accepted a knighthood from the Caribbean state of Antigua and Barbuda. He decorated his offices with hunting prints and sponsored a polo championship at Sandhurst in which Prince Harry played. Despite his Texan origins, he was best known in Britain for his sponsorship of cricket; he built his own ground in Antigua and funded a Twenty20 cricket series in the West Indies, culminating in the 2008 match between England and a Stanford Superstars team. He even acquired an English girlfriend, who came from Dartford. But Stanford never quite made it as an Englishman. Arriving at Lords in a helicopter with a chest containing $20 million in new bills and being pictured cavorting with the wives and girlfriends of English test cricketers did not endear him to the British press.

Because they were outsiders, status and reputation were important to all these men. Becoming wealthy made them socially acceptable and this made it easier for them to attract new victims. As well as adopting English pursuits, Stanford tried to enhance his credibility in the USA by demonstrating that he had inherited wealth. He claimed that his father had left him an insurance business with 500 employees and employed genealogists to prove that he was descended from a relative of Leland Stanford, who had founded Stanford University in California. The university was not wholly convinced by this connection and at one stage brought an action against him for infringement of copyright.

Being known to possess old money helped deflect potential questions about who precisely was investing in Stanford's early enterprises. He lived a life of extreme luxury, with two yachts and he owned Tyecliffe Castle, a 57-room mock-castle in a Miami suburb, as well as a mansion in St Croix in the US Virgin Islands. Stanford was no fool and being able to show that he had inherited money and that he had close links with the polo and cricket establishments must have helped him to demonstrate to potential clients that he was a decent chap – one who could be trusted with their life savings.

Dickens said of his fictional con man, Mr Merdle, in *Little Dorrit*:

Mr Merdle was immensely rich; a man of prodigious enterprise; a Midas without the ears who turned all he touched to gold. He was in everything good, from banking to building. He was in Parliament, of course. He was in the City, necessarily. He was Chairman of this, Trustee of that, President of the other ... It was heresy to regard [Mr Merdle] as anything less than all of the British merchants since [Dick] Whittington rolled into one and gilded three feet deep all over.

In *Martin Chuzzlewit* fraudster Tigg Montague gradually becomes richer and more important: 'Mr Tigg ... had really risen with his opportunities and, peculating on a grander scale, he had become a grander man altogether'. Eventually, he sets himself up in a fine set of rooms and founds a company to which he gave a splendid title – The Anglo-Bengalee Disinterested Loan and Life Assurance Company. He claims to own a large property in Bengal, which is available to support all claims on the company. He says, 'It is a devilish fine property to be amenable to any claims. The preserve of tigers alone is worth a mint of money'. Dr Jopling sells Montague's insurance policies to his patients and says he was: 'A remarkable handsome man, and quite the gentleman in every respect. Property I am told in India. House and everything belong to him, beautiful. Costly furniture on the most elegant and lavish scale'.

Tigg Montague's business in *Martin Chuzzlewit* has sometimes been seen as the first example of a Ponzi scheme, although it also seems to have included elements of a modern payday loan company. Tigg explains how it works. A man referred to as B, who might be a small tradesman, clerk, parson, artist, author or have any other profession, is hard up and in desperate need of a loan:

> *Say £50 or £100; perhaps more; no matter. B proposes self and two securities, B is accepted. Two securities give a bond. B assures his own life for double the amount and brings two friends' lives also – just to patronize the office ... besides charging B the regular interest, we get B's premium, and B's friends premiums, and we charge B for the bond, and whether we accept him or not we charge B for inquiries (we keep a man, at a pound a week, to make 'em) and we charge B a trifle for the secretary and in short my good fellow, we stick it into B, up hill and down dale, and make a devilish comfortable little property out of him.*

John Sadleir marked his rising status and prosperity by buying large estates in Ireland. The great famine of 1845–1847 had left Irish agriculture in a terrible condition; many people had died or emigrated. A large number of landowners were in difficulties, deeply in debt and unable to meet their obligations. In 1848 the Encumbered Estates Court was set up to allow the sale of mortgaged properties. An owner, or someone with a claim on the estate could apply for it to be sold and the court would arrange a sale and distribute the proceeds amongst the creditors. The essential idea of the court was to attract new capital from England to revitalize Irish agriculture.

Sadleir took full advantage of these opportunities and he spent £233,000 acquiring 30,000 acres in Tipperary, Cork, Waterford, Mayo, Galway, Kerry, Limerick and Roscommon. Some of his land purchases were funded by debt; he borrowed £52,000 from a relative, Thomas J. Eyre to fund his purchase of the Glengall Estate. As well as his landed ventures, he opened a newspaper, *The Telegraph*, which sold a million copies at its peak. He also became involved in a gold mining company and in railways in Sweden and Kent – his company was responsible for the first railway bridge over the Medway at Rochester. Finally, to seal his place in the British establishment, he loaned £90,000 to a duke – the deeply indebted Duke of Buckingham. As Alex Dalmady said of Allen Stanford over a century later, these investments – a gold mine; a couple of railway companies which had not yet completed their lines; extensive landed estates; and a large loan to a failing aristocrat – appear more like a rich man's playthings than genuine businesses.

Ponzi had only a little time in the limelight before his scheme came crashing down, but he too marked his importance by conspicuous expenditure. He bought two fine motor cars, a large house with a swimming pool and air conditioning in addition to gaining control of a bank and a company called J.R. Poole, which was in the meat and fish canning business. Like Sadleir and Stanford, Ponzi's investments looked frivolous. In particular the investment in J.R. Poole seems like an act of mere childishness. J.R. Poole had employed him as a junior clerk years before and Ponzi wanted to show how far he had come since those days.

In contrast, Madoff was already a Wall Street legend with all the status that implied; he served four terms on the Board of Governors of the National Association of Securities Dealers and became Chair of the NASDAQ market. He lived a lavish lifestyle as a member of country clubs and an owner of properties in New York, Long Island, Florida and the Cap d'Antibes in the south of France. As late as 2007, when it must have been obvious that things were not going to last much longer, he bought a half-share in a business jet and a yacht; he also treated his brother to a vintage Aston Martin.

Like many on Wall Street, he was involved in charities, particularly those run by his leading investors. He was a significant supporter of a home for performing arts in New York called the New York City Center. He was not entirely cynical in his charitable activities, however, and the death of his nephew Roger from leukaemia led him to support the Gift of Life Bone Marrow Foundation which finds bone marrow matches for adults with leukaemia, while his son Andrew's battle with lymphoma persuaded Madoff to give millions to the Lymphoma Research Foundation. Much of this generosity was, of course, carried out with other people's money.

Most of our confidence tricksters demonstrated some previous evidence of poor behaviour. Dickens shows Tigg Montague also committing minor misdemeanours: failing to pay his hotel bills and general arrogance. Mark Tapley, barman and general hand at the Blue Dragon reported that,

Him and his friend goes and stops at the Moon and Stars till they've run up a bill there; and then comes and stops with us and does the same. The running of bills is common enough; it ain't that as we object to; it's the ways of this chap. Nothing's good enough for him; all the women is

dying for him he thinks and is overpaid if he winks at 'em and all the men was made to be ordered about by him.

Irish landowner, John Sadleir, seems to have indulged in a tendency to criminal behaviour from an early stage in his career. He provided mortgages to impoverished estates, but sometimes cheated their owners by issuing them with forged receipts, and he also acquired property by fraudulent means. Throughout his life he behaved dishonestly, cheating Sir George and Lady Clara Goold out of their marriage settlement and even having a political opponent, Edmund Downing falsely arrested for debt at the time of the 1852 general election. His whole business was based on a lie. He ran the Tipperary Bank without proper audits and borrowed large sums from it. By 1856 he realized that the situation was unsustainable; he could no longer afford to pay his debts to the bank and the bank itself was rapidly running out of money.

As a desperate measure, he proposed marriage to several wealthy heiresses, but they all turned him down and his doom was inescapable. We are never told about the past misbehaviours of Sadleir's fictional equivalent, Mr Merdle, but Dickens implies that those close to him are aware of his failings. After his suicide, his chief butler comments, 'Mr Merdle never was the gentleman and no ungentlemanly act on Mr Merdle's part would surprise me'.

Unlike his fellows, William '520 per cent' Miller seems to have had no previous form. He was a young Brooklyn bookkeeper, who in 1899 fleeced many savers out of their money in a proto-Ponzi scheme. He began in a quiet way in March of that year, persuading fellow members of his church to invest small amounts of money with him and offering a return of 10 per cent a week (or 520 per cent a year). He claimed that he was able to do this because he had insider information about events on the stock exchange.

At first his business was tiny, but gradually more people joined and he began to advertise, calling his scheme the Franklin Syndicate. By October and November he was taking in between $20,000 and $63,000 a day and it is estimated that he stole about $1.2 million from the public. When Miller fled, the United States Post Office found that it had undelivered letters to him containing $100,000 dollars in cash intended for investment in the syndicate.

Ponzi had a much more overtly criminal career behind him; sacked from a job as a waiter for short-changing customers and stealing. He then worked for Luigi Zarossi, who was running a banking scam within a bank for Italian immigrants. After Zarossi fled to Mexico, Ponzi tried to help his family, but he was desperately short of money and forged a cheque for $423, for which he was caught and sentenced to three years in prison. He then got involved in smuggling Italians across the border with Canada and spent a further two years in jail.

Madoff too had some previous form. In 1960 he began acting as a broker in the Over the Counter market selling newly issued shares to a small group of relatives and friends. He was probably acting illegally because not all these new issues were suitable for inexperienced share-holders. Unfortunately for him, in May 1962 the market witnessed its biggest fall since 1929 and many of the shares he had bought for his clients collapsed. Rather than admit to the losses, he borrowed money from his father-in-law and bought back the shares from his clients at the same price at which he had sold them. Clearly he was demon-strating an early skill in bamboozling people and a disregard for honesty and transparency. However, the fact that he was a rare example of a lucky 'hot issue boy' who escaped the 1962 crash con-tributed to his reputation for financial genius, although we only have his account of this event and the truth cannot now be established.

Madoff was soon back in business and continued to operate in the same way, using his father-in-law's firm and its successor as feeder funds. They raised the money and passed it to Madoff, who invested it. He was interested in technology at an early stage and in 1970 his brother Peter joined the firm and oversaw its computerization, joining the newly created NASDAQ electronic share dealing system. Madoff always had two sides to his business, a legitimate brokerage business, which bought and sold stocks on behalf of clients, and a huge money management business. Madoff kept the two businesses quite separate, operating the dodgy business from a separate floor in the same building. Many of his employees, including his two sons, worked in the legitimate side of the business; Mark Madoff joined in 1987 and his younger son Andrew in 1989, career choices they would eventually come to bitterly regret.

Despite energetic inquiries by investigative journalists, it seems that Stanford was an exception to this rule, at least in his earliest years. He ran a gym in Waco, Texas, which failed, but nowadays many success-ful entrepreneurs have a track record of failed businesses before hitting on a winner. However, his activities after the gym failed are more questionable. The financial downturn that had ruined his gym also had a bad effect on the Texas property market and he went into business with his father, buying properties from owners in financial trouble and also began building houses.

In 1985 Stanford opened a small bank on the island of Montserrat. Quite how he funded these activities is not known; his father had a small insurance business which he sold and the money from the sale may have helped, but it cannot have provided enough funds for a property development business or a bank. Also, while the property business might have made money in the long run, house prices in Texas remained depressed for years. There were stories about South American connections and it seems that many of his investors came from that part of the world.

The bank was initially successful and by 1990 it had $55 million in deposits, but the Montserrat authorities had serious concerns about it. They were worried that his bank had a bankrupt as a director (Stanford had not declared his bankruptcy), that it did not supply sufficient information about liquidity, that its auditor was not an approved bank auditor and there were also concerns about the sources of his funding. In order to avoid having his banking licence revoked, he moved his business to Antigua and Barbuda. He soon became a major force there, lending money to the government and politicians, buying newspapers and developing holiday resorts and restaurants.

One of the traits linking these con men is their use of similar psychological techniques to persuade their victims to sign up. One favoured method was to make their schemes seem very attractive by making it appear very hard for people to invest in them. Dickens understood this approach very clearly. Part of the plot of *Little Dorrit* concerns John Dorrit, who had spent long years in the Marshalsea Prison as a debtor, but eventually came into a fortune and was released. Naturally he asked the great financier Mr Merdle if he could help him to invest his newly acquired money. Mr Merdle replied:

> *It would not be at the present moment easy for what I may call a mere outsider to come into any of the good things – unless at a high price. At what we are accustomed to term a very long figure. However, I do generally retain in my own hands the power of exercising some preference – people in general would be pleased to call it favour – as a sort of complement for my care and trouble ... I will see, if you please, how I can exert this limited power (for people are jealous and it is limited) to your advantage ... Of course there must be the strictest integrity and uprightness*

in these transactions; there must be the purest faith between man and man … therefore I can only give you a preference to a certain extent.

Tigg Montague also uses a similar approach. He employs a doctor, Dr Jobling, to examine people wishing to take out a policy with his company. Dr Jobling's main role seems to have been to impress potential customers with the difficulty of getting into the Anglo-Bengalee and he makes a great show of 'feeling their pulses, looking at their tongues, listening at their ribs, poking them in the chest and so forth'. In fact, as Jopling well knew, the Anglo-Bengalee would accept any customer at all.

Later, Montague's associate, Jonas Chuzzlewit tries to persuade his father-in-law, Mr Pecksniff, to become a partner in the company. His method is similar – he deliberately behaves in a surly manner towards Pecksniff and Pecksniff naturally thinks, 'If this young man wanted anything of me for his own ends, he would be polite and deferential. The more Jonas repelled him in his hints and inquiries, the more solicitous therefore, Mr Pecksniff came to be initiated into the golden mysteries he had obscurely glanced'.

David Sarna has commented that one of Madoff's strengths was that he made it difficult for people to get into his business; he turned down some investors and others had to wait years before they were admitted. If Madoff took your money, it was a sign you had arrived and it was simply impolite to ask too many questions. In the early days, Madoff was very secretive. His main source of funds was a company called Avellino and Bienes, who took money from investors and then reinvested with Madoff. In 1990 they wrote to an inquirer: 'We do not encourage new accounts and therefore we do not solicit same. Summarily this is a very private group and no financial statements, prospectuses or brochures have been printed or are available'.

Elie Wiesel, the holocaust survivor and Nobel prize-winner was one of Madoff's victims – he lost his life savings and the funds of his charity. He described the world in which Madoff worked:

I remember that it was a myth that he created round him. That everything was so special, so unique; that it had to be secret … It was like a mystical mythology that nobody could understand. Just as the myth of exclusivity, he gave the impression that maybe a hundred people belonged to his club. Now we know he cheated thousands of them.

As well as making people enthusiastic to join these exclusive clubs, creating obstacles to signing up had a couple of other advantages.

First, it made it much less likely that people would ask awkward questions. After all, nobody admitted to an exclusive London club once having been nominated and vetted by the committee would go and inspect the kitchens. Second, it hid the true scale of the business. This was particularly important for Madoff, but also applied to many of our other fraudsters because the mathematics of their schemes simply didn't work. Had Elie Wiesel known that thousands of other people were getting exclusive access to Madoff's skills, then he might have thought twice about investing with him.

* * *

Ponzi schemes cannot continue because they cannot go on for long attracting enough victims to keep paying the dividends to existing investors. Dickens explained this in *Martin Chuzzlewit*: Tigg Montague sold life assurance policies and Jonas Chuzzlewit asked him what happened when people die. Montague replied that at the start they had a couple of unlucky deaths and he had to pawn all the furniture except a grand piano, 'and it was an upright-grand too so that I couldn't even sit upon it'. He soon got back into business, but he admitted to Jonas that, if a lot of people died and he would be faced with huge payments, then the only option left to him would be to bolt.

Ponzi quickly got himself into a position where bolting was the only sensible option. This is because his business was totally unsustainable. He offered unbelievable rates of interest: 50 per cent in 45 days, whereas normal banks offered five per cent a year. He claimed to be able to offer these crazy rates because, as we have seen, he was exploiting the different prices at which international reply coupons could be purchased in Europe and the price at which they could be redeemed in the USA. So attractive were his rates that many thousands of people flocked to invest with him and he eventually received many millions of dollars from investors.

Clarence Barron, a famous financial commentator, was commissioned by the *Boston Post* to investigate Ponzi's scheme. Barron pointed out that, in order to cover the money paid in by investors in the company, 160 million international reply coupons would have had to have been in circulation. In fact, only 27,000 were available and the United States Post Office reported that International Reply Coupons were not being bought in large quantities either at home or abroad. Moreover, as Barron pointed out, the potential profit on buying international coupons abroad and then cashing them in the USA would have been eaten up by the costs of handling millions of individual coupons.

By the time Sir Allen Stanford began his activities, people had become more financially aware and there was a greater range of information available in the newspapers and better advice, notably that if a thing seems too good to be true, it probably is. Consequently, he had to be careful not to make very exaggerated claims. His main financial products were certificates of deposit, which were interest-paying deposits in his bank. He offered rates of just over 5 per cent for a three-year certificate compared with just over 3 per cent in a normal US bank. This was enough to attract customers, but not high enough to cause suspicions, particularly as he explained that his rates were good because he paid low taxes in Antigua and had good underlying investments. He implied that they were guaranteed by the US Securities Investor Protection Corporation, which had been set up by the US Congress to protect brokerage customers. He also claimed that purchasers of his certificates of deposit were protected by an insurance policy at Lloyds of London, but in 2007, this policy, which was for $100 million covered less than 2 per cent of the total outstanding deposits.

Stanford was unusual in that his business activities were pretty constantly under investigation by the US Securities and Exchange Commission, but for many years nothing was done, despite pressure from junior staff. There have been suggestions that he was protected by the American Drug Enforcement Agency because he was working on their behalf and it is certainly true that the Venezuelan military intelligence raided his offices in Caracas in 2008, claiming that some of his employees were paid by the CIA to act as spies. The story is very murky and the full details have not yet been revealed.

Perhaps a more likely explanation for the failure of the regulators to act is the complexity of Stanford's business. Stanford's main investment products were certificates of deposit. These are very common in the United States and are simply fixed-term investment products, usually with a fixed interest rate and very like the fixed term bonds or savings accounts offered by British banks and building societies. Savers agree to commit their money for a longer period in return for a slightly higher rate of interest; there are usually penalties for early withdrawal or closure of the account.

Stanford sold certificates of deposit to American citizens through his bank based in the Caribbean state of Antigua and Barbuda. As the bank was not based in the United States, it was not regulated by the US authorities. The certificates were not issued by an American bank and so some regulators believed that US banking laws did not apply. Nor were the securities like stocks and shares and consequently it was felt that US securities laws did not apply either. The financial regulators in the USA like to go for easy, uncomplicated wins and in Stanford's case they may have backed away because the matter was complex and offered no immediate prospects of success. While Stanford had been under suspicion at various times since the 1980s, it was not until 2009, when his empire was reeling from the shock of the 2008 financial crash, that the US regulators finally acted.

What is certainly true is that the mortal blow to the Stanford empire was not struck by well-paid US financial regulators, but by Alex Dalmady, who began to investigate Stanford's banking empire as a favour to a friend who was one of Stanford's clients. In his article, 'Duck Tales', he used freely available online sources and came to some startling conclusions: the bank was offering very high rates of interest – 7.5 per cent, as opposed to the 4.5 per cent US banks were offering. It had grown very quickly, from $624 million deposits in 1999 to $8.4 billion in 2008. Rapid growth in deposits is a bad sign in banks, showing that something may be 'too attractive.'

The high returns that the bank was making were consistent even in bad years; Dalmady described them as being on the 'limit of the credible universe'. Some of its publicly acknowledged investments – a resort development business, three movies, a golf club manufacturer, a golf course, an auction house and a restaurant in Memphis – seemed to him more like millionaires' toys than investments. There was only one board member, an 85-year-old former cattle rancher and used car dealership owner. The auditor was a local island firm, whose principal was 72 years old and had been auditing the bank for many years. His conclusion was that Stanford's bank was a duck. Dalmady's ideas were picked up on the internet and eventually published in the US financial magazine *Business Week*. Stanford's ship began sinking beneath the Caribbean.

Madoff was much more subtle than Ponzi or Stanford. Although he was running a scam, he was careful to ensure that the profits he declared and the returns he gave to investors did not seem excessive. In fact his returns were no better than those on a go-getting unit trust, but Madoff offered consistency. During the boom year of 1982, some investors turned to him because they valued the steady returns he offered which were unlike the rollercoaster ride provided by the market. Unfortunately for Madoff, he had a rival – an organisation called the Gateway Fund, which used the same investment techniques. This fund was never able to produce the same predictable returns that Madoff delivered.

Consequently, people began to get suspicious. Their suspicions grew as Madoff's business prospered. A number of investment experts felt that if Madoff was really operating in the way he claimed, and buying the numbers of shares and options required to sustain his business, then there would be evidence of his activities in the market, but there simply wasn't. In 2001 Erin E. Arvelund published an article in *Barrons* magazine called 'Don't Ask, Don't Tell' questioning Madoff's remarkably consistent investment performance.

Madoff had a nasty moment in October 1987, when on 'Black Monday' the market fell by nearly a quarter, twice as much as the worst day of the 1929 Wall Street crash. Madoff's technology helped him survive the crash, but some of his big clients started to withdraw funds and Madoff began to have serious cash-flow problems to cover these redemptions. Madoff said at his trial that his Ponzi scheme began in 1991. The problems following the 1987 crash and the withdrawal of investments, which left him owing several billions of dollars, may have first driven him to dip into clients' funds. He claimed that he always had intended to resume legitimate trading but it proved too difficult and ultimately impossible.

In 1992 he faced a further crisis when the Securities and Exchange Commission (SEC) raided Avellino and Bienes and found that they had been accepting loans totalling about $400 million from clients and investing the money with Madoff. They checked that Madoff still had the money and examined his accounts. They then demanded that he refund the investments to Avellino and Bienes. Madoff dealt with these problems in ways that would become characteristic of his business activities. He produced false accounts to show that the money was still in place and 'borrowed' the money from a client account to repay Avellino and Bienes.

His business was simply a Ponzi scheme; Madoff banked the money he received from investors and when somebody wanted their money repaid, he simply paid them out of the account. Like all good Ponzi schemes it could only keep going while new money flowed in. He went to some lengths to convince doubting investors and investigators that the money had genuinely been invested in stocks and shares.

Once Madoff had bought shares, they were deposited with the Depository Trust and Clearing Corporation for safekeeping. In order to convince sceptics that he had made huge investments with their money, he set up a computer screen, purportedly an exact replica of the Depository Trust's screen. Investors were shown this screen with records of the billions of shares that he had deposited. Madoff believed that he could have been caught in 2003, if an SEC investigator had bothered to check with the Depository Trust Corporation.

Important investors were given an even bigger treat. When Jeffrey Tucker of Fairfield Greenwich visited, he was shown an entirely bogus computer terminal made to appear as if it were dealing with Europe. In fact, it was linked to a technician in the next room. All this was overseen by Madoff's auditors – a single company with just one qualified auditor.

Madoff's biggest critic was Harry Markopolos who, in 1999, was asked by his employers to design a product to enable them to compete with Madoff. After some investigations, Markopolos concluded that Madoff's scheme was phoney. His returns were simply too consistent – they did not track the way the market moved. The fund was also too big not to have had an effect on the market as a whole. Madoff claimed that he was buying options to cover his trades, but to do this he would have had to buy more options than actually existed. Moreover, although his fund was worth about $6 billion by then, there was no evidence that his trades had any impact on the market.

In May 2001, Michael Ocrant wrote an article in the *MarHedge* financial newsletter supporting Markopolos. The article stated that experts had argued that Madoff's returns were too high and too consistent. Markopolos persistently drew the attention of the SEC to his views on Madoff and was consistently ignored. His final effort came in 2005, when he sent a 21-page document to the SEC baldly entitled 'The World's Largest Hedge Fund is a Fraud'. He provided much evidence that Madoff's business was fake, including the fact that over the past 14 years, Madoff's fund had only had four losing months; impossible for such a large player in the stock market. Markopolos later published a book, *No One Would Listen: a True Financial Thriller*, a remarkable indictment of the failure of the US authorities to act on the mounting evidence against Madoff.

Other con men were also suspected of being up to no good long before they were caught, but the suspicious either kept their views to themselves or were ignored. James Sadleir told his brother John that he considered him quite incapable and unfit to run the banking business – 18 months before the Sadleir business blew up. In *Martin Chuzzlewit*, Dr Jopling clearly has his doubts about the Anglo-Bengalee Company:

'Caution is my weak side, that's the truth and always was from a boy. That is,' said the doctor filling his glass, 'caution in behalf of other people. Whether I would repose confidence in this company myself if I had not been paying money elsewhere for many years, that's quite another question'. He tried to look as if there were no doubt about it; but feeling that he did it but indifferently, changed the theme and praised the wine.

The authorities seemed to have been suspicious of William Miller from the start. US Post Office Inspector William S. McGuinness had Miller's syndicate under observation for several weeks, but could find no evidence on which to proceed against him. He wrote 250 letters to Miller's customers in various parts of the United States, asking them if they had any complaints to make. Yet, all the replies expressed satisfaction with Miller. The local police had the same problem. Captain James Reynolds of the Brooklyn Police Department found that nobody was prepared to speak against Miller and the people in his neighbourhood all had faith in him and many of the merchants there continued to honour his cheques.

Ponzi began his scheme in December 1919 and fairly shortly afterwards he came to the notice of Berry Benson of Augusta, Georgia. Benson was a Confederate War veteran, who was well-known in Augusta for serving as the model for the statue of the enlisted soldier on the Confederate War Memorial, as well as championing good causes and being a shrewd accountant. Benson had already alerted the authorities to the fact that it was possible to buy francs cheaply in France and change them at the official rate in the US. He recognized Ponzi's scheme as something questionable and contacted the Massachusetts attorney general. Local newspapers in Augusta credited Benson with being the man who initiated the investigation which led to Ponzi's downfall but in fact there is little evidence that he was taken seriously. It was not until April 1920 that the police and post office officials began to take notice. For several months they did not quite seem to know whether a crime was being committed and, if so, what it was.

* * *

In a nice judgement of fate, nearly all these con men came to terrible ends. Sadleir faced ruin in February 1856 when Glyn's bank, his London agent refused to process drafts from his Tipperary Bank and a run began on several branches of the bank, which managed to keep going until closing time on the following Saturday. Sadleir desperately tried to raise additional loans, but none were forthcoming.

On the Saturday evening, he sent his butler to buy a bottle of essential oil of bitter almonds (prussic acid or hydrogen cyanide) from a chemist. He wrote four letters confessing his guilt and dressed splendidly in a fancy shirt, black silk neckerchief, raised silk plush waistcoat, fancy tweed trousers, a frock coat, a black hat from Christie's of Bond Street and a pair of buckskin gloves. He walked across Hampstead Heath to the grassy area behind Jack Straw's Castle and drank the poison, mixed with sugar and opium, from a silver cream jug. His body was found the next morning and was identified by Edwin James QC MP and Thomas Wakley MP, editor of *The Lancet*. Because he had committed suicide, Sadleir could not be buried in consecrated ground, and consequently he was laid to rest in Highgate Cemetery.

Sadleir's brother James suffered an even stranger fate; after John's death, he attempted a complex legal manoeuvre to protect his own interests in the Tipperary Bank. The Irish Master of the Rolls called it one of the most monstrous propositions he had ever heard. He was later indicted on eight counts of fraud and conspiracy and fled abroad. He first went to Denmark, then Paris, Boulogne and finally Zurich where, abandoned by his wife, he lived on an annuity from her family. In 1881 he was murdered during an attempted robbery while out for an afternoon stroll.

Dickens imagined an equally dramatic ending for Mr Merdle in *Little Dorrit*. He knows that his business is facing ruin, so he borrows a penknife with a tortoiseshell handle and goes to the local bathhouse, where his body is later found in a bath. 'On the ledge next to the bath were an empty laudanum bottle and a tortoise-shell handled penknife – soiled, but not with ink'. Like Sadleir, Merdle's body is identified by a doctor and a lawyer.

John Sadleir's life was like a Greek tragedy – the hero being punished for hubris and dying in the last act. His dramatic tale inspired a number of writers, including, as we have seen, Charles Dickens. In Joseph Hatton's version of the story, Sadleir has a double, whom he murders and dumps on Hampstead Heath and flees to America, where he is eventually arrested and commits suicide. The idea that the body on the Heath was not Sadleir's is not just a figment of Hatton's imagination, but was mentioned by newspapers of the day. The novelist Mary Elizabeth Bradden portrayed Sadleir as 'Jabez North' and her fictional account of his career, *The Trail of the Serpent* included infanticide, the murders of an old man and a pregnant woman and finally a gruesome death in a prison cell.

Dickens's other great financial villain, Tigg Montague, also suffers a gruesome death in *Martin Chuzzlewit*. He brings Jonas Chuzzlewit into partnership, knowing that Jonas planned to murder his own father. Gradually he begins to put the squeeze on Jonas, making him undertake difficult tasks for the business but not handing over a just share of the rewards. Enraged, Jonas murders Tigg in a wood. Jonas is eventually arrested for his murder but manages to poison himself before he can be tried.

Ponzi also came to an unfortunate end. Once it became obvious that his business was doomed, he surrendered to the authorities and was charged and convicted for mail fraud – a federal offence. He was imprisoned and released in 1922. The Massachusetts authorities then charged him with 22 counts of larceny. After an appeal to the Supreme Court and three separate criminal trials he was convicted, but released on bail pending an appeal.

Ponzi fled to Florida, where he set up a new fraudulent scheme, the Charpon Land Syndicate, offering investors small parcels of swamp land guaranteeing them a return of 200 per cent in 60 days. He was arrested, convicted and sentenced to a year in a Florida prison. However, Ponzi fled bail, grew a moustache and shaved his head and got a job on a ship bound for Italy. Unfortunately, the ship subsequently called at New Orleans, where he was arrested and sent back to Boston to serve his sentence.

Having endured two periods of imprisonment in the US, Ponzi was then deported to Italy. He struggled to find work but eventually got a job with the airline Ala Littoria and was appointed as their agent in Brazil. During the Second World War, Brazil joined the Allies. As a result Italian businesses in the country were closed down, including Ponzi's employer, leaving him jobless. He spent his remaining years in poverty, relying on occasional work as a translator before he died in 1949.

Ponzi was totally unrepentant even in his last interview, when he said, 'Even if they never got anything for it, it was cheap at that price. Without malice aforethought I had given them the best show that was ever staged in their territory since the landing of the Pilgrims! It was easily worth 15 million bucks to watch me put the thing over'.

The end of Bernie Madoff was quite extraordinary. By December 2008 he was aware that, because of the financial crisis, his Ponzi scheme could no longer be sustained. He confessed to his brother Peter and then told his two sons Mark and Andrew. They immediately went to a lawyer, Martin Flumenbaum, who contacted the US Attorney's Office in New York and the Securities and Exchange Commission. According to Barbara Henriques, when Flumenbaum telephoned the SEC, he told his contact that Madoff's losses could amount to 50 billion. His contact asked 'Is that billion with a B?' That night was Madoff's annual Christmas party at a Mexican restaurant. Madoff and his wife attended, their sons did not. The next day, Madoff was arrested and in March 2009 pleaded guilty to 11 felonies. He was sentenced to 150 years in prison, but has suffered further punishment since; his son Mark committed suicide in 2010, and he has become estranged from his other son.

Stanford seems to have escaped somewhat more lightly. While on remand he was subject to a severe beating by fellow prisoners and became addicted to prescription drugs. Having been stripped of his knighthood and convicted, he was sentenced to 110 years in prison.

The only con man who seems to have had a relatively happy ending was the notorious William '520 percent' Miller, whose financial scheme had been one of Ponzi's inspirations. In November 1899 it was obvious that the game was up and Miller's business associate, Edward Schlesinger, took his share of the cash, probably about $145,000 and fled to Europe. There were many rumours about his whereabouts, including stories that he was living in Paris, or Baden Baden or hiding out in New York. Miller's lawyer, Robert A. Ammon, then persuaded Miller to give him all his money – probably about $240,000, because, as attorney for Miller, Ammon was protected by privilege, so even if Miller were punished for the fraud, the creditors would never see their money again. The next day, Miller learned that he was about to be arrested and escaped a detective by dodging through a drug store and a Chinese laundry, eventually escaping to Canada, where he was arrested and sentenced to 10 years in Sing Sing.

Miller's lawyer, Ammon, was concerned about being implicated in the Franklin Syndicate and so he agreed to pay $5 a week to Miller's wife and child in return for Miller's silence. Three years later, Miller changed his mind and made a full confession. He admitted that the Franklin Syndicate was a fraud from the start; the money he received from investors was never invested; it was simply kept in a safe in his office. All he ever did was to change small denomination bills for larger ones when the safe was getting full. As a result of Miller's testimony, his lawyer Ammon was convicted of theft and sentenced to four and a half years' imprisonment.

In 1920, at the height of the Ponzi scandal, the *New York Evening World* tracked Miller down. By then, he had put his life of crime behind him. Having served five years in prison, he had bought a small grocery store in Rockville Center, Long Island. When the newspaper interviewed him, he said 'I may be rather dense, but I cannot understand how Ponzi made so much money in so short a time'. He said that he would not take $10 million to be in Ponzi's shoes if Ponzi was behaving dishonestly. He said he was happy with his life owning a small grocery store, having few worries and breathing God's free pure country air.

J.K. Galbraith, the Harvard economist, believed that the volume of financial fraud (which he called 'the bezzle' from the word embezzlement) increases in good times because auditors and investors become more confident, whereas it falls in lean years as they become more cautious. Speaking at a panel meeting to discuss Madoff in 2009, James Chanos said:

> *As the financial juices get flowing, as they were a few years ago, we begin to suspend disbelief in what normally would be a situation where one would equate risk with reward, and would be sceptical of anything that appears too good to be true. When everybody's making money, it's very easy to set that aside.*

Both Stanford and Madoff prospered in the good years up to 2008, but as the economy collapsed the fault lines in their businesses became more prominent. Stanford had invested heavily in property in Florida, one of the areas worst affected by the 2008 financial collapse. What is alarming is that, despite the enormous amount of money spent on financial regulation and policing, none of these crooks were caught by the regulators and most only came to public attention because their schemes collapsed under their own weight. It is perhaps worth considering how many other undetected schemes might still be in operation.

One of the most intriguing questions is the extent to which these men are villains and the extent to which they are merely self-delusional. Many of them seem to have happily robbed their own families as well as thousands of other people. The crash of the Sadleir enterprise brought losses to many of his relatives; not only did they lose the money they had invested with him, but also, as shareholders, they were liable for a share of the debts of the bank. Robert Keating, a cousin, lost his job at the London and County Bank because of his Sadleir connections; he also gave up his seat in parliament and had to sell his family property of Garranlea, in the family since 1783. Another cousin, John Ryan, had to pay £1,500 as a result of his investment, give up the mastership of a famous pack of hounds, and rely on the benevolence of a neighbour until he got back on his feet. Two other relatives fled to Paris to escape their creditors.

Dickens's two fictional villains are both quite willing to steal from their families. Mr Merdle's stepson has just married Mr Doritt's daughter, but Merdle is happy to encourage Doritt to invest all his money in a fraudulent scheme. Similarly, the villainous Jonas Chuzzle-wit persuades his father-in-law to invest in Tigg Montague's fake insurance business. Mrs Ponzi's family were not wealthy, but Charles Ponzi was happy to take their money and, in total, he borrowed $16,075 (roughly £120,000 today) from them.

Madoff took money from his family, his wife's relatives, his employees and friends; he had used his network of contacts to attract likely investors. When he was arrested, the judge insisted that he should find four people to act as sureties for him. He could only find two – his wife and brother. He could not turn to his friends, who were also his victims, while his sons were unwilling to help and their lawyers had advised them not to. Consequently, Madoff had to submit to tagging and home detention, or as one comic said, 'penthouse arrest'.

Not only did these men do huge damage to their families, but they also caused much pain and financial loss to thousands of innocent people. Sadleir's victims included: Richard O'Flaherty, a farmer from Killusty, who lost £2,180; Thomas Blake, the parish priest of Roscrea, lost £182; while the Tipperary Chapel fund lost £2,400. Even those who had nothing to do with Sadleir suffered; the Nenagh Poor Law Union lost money with Sadleir and an old man, Simon Armstrong, who had guaranteed the union funds was unable to pay his security and was prosecuted by the Nenagh Board and apparently imprisoned.

Eventually, after sterling work by the official appointed to oversee Sadleir's finances, money was recovered and people received about a third of the money they had lost, but they had to wait 25 years for the final payment.

Ponzi also caused much financial hardship to his victims; he cheerfully took an investment of $600 from a priest – a fund collected for repainting the priest's church. In the end, his victims were also repaid about a third of their losses.

Dickens presents a dramatic picture of the consequences of Merdle's ruin. Early in the morning, after he has committed suicide, his doctor hurries round to a friend, who is a lawyer, and shows him the suicide note in which Merdle confesses that his business is ruined. The two men think, 'If all those hundreds and thousands of beggared people who were yet asleep, could only know, as they two spoke, the ruin that impended over them, what a fearful cry against one miserable soul would go up to heaven'.

William Miller's victims lost a significant amount of their investments and some were very badly affected. Among them was Mrs Augusta Cooke of Paterson New Jersey, a widow who had been left $1,000 by her husband, with which she had planned to set up a girls' school. Unfortunately, she entrusted half of it to Miller and was forced to go back to her old job as a stenographer.

Claims totalling $11.9 billion have been submitted to the liquidator of Madoff's estate by his creditors and it seems likely that a substantial proportion of these will be met. However, not all the investors are happy; the liquidator is only paying out what they originally invested minus any money they had withdrawn. Some still hoped to get the fanciful returns Madoff had promised them, while others wanted additional interest because they had invested their money with Madoff for a long period of time. Sadly, two of Madoff's victims, the financier René-Thierry Magon de la Villehuchet and the British army officer Major William Foxton both committed suicide when faced with financial ruin.

Stanford's victims fared worse than those of Madoff. Because his bank had been based in Antigua they were not able to claim compensation from the US financial compensation scheme and the receiver has had a hard time raising very much money from the remaining assets. In May 2013, a US court authorized an interim payment of $55 million, just 1 per cent of Stanford's debts.

As well as causing huge distress to individuals, some of these schemes did a lot of collateral damage to other companies. As a result of Sadleir's dishonesty, the Carson's Creek Gold Mining Company and the Royal Swedish Railway faced ruin, as did the Tipperary Bank and the Newcastle Bank, though a few of his businesses were lucky; the East Kent Railway survived and continued to develop the line. Ponzi's failure led to the collapse of a number of banks, including the Hanover, the Tremont and the Polish Industrial Association Bank. All these failures led to people losing their jobs or their savings and sometimes both.

Indeed, although the perpetrators of Ponzi schemes caused terrible damage to their victims, it is clear that both victims and villains had much in common with each other. The investors in the various schemes described appear to have believed that it was possible to achieve wholly incredible returns on their money and that somehow it was possible to earn much more than the normal return from investing in the stock market.

This is a common fallacy, as Evan Newmark wrote in *The New York Times*, 'The belief that one can beat the market is the core operating principle of Wall Street. It is the philosophical grease that keeps all the machines of Wall Street humming'. In fact, many professional investors struggle to even keep up with the market, which is why there is currently a trend for buying index tracker funds that guarantee to keep their value in line with the main market indices. Some of these con men were as optimistic and unrealistic as the people they tricked. John Sadleir was a persistent speculator in shares and commodities. In 1855, he claimed that he had lost £120,000 in sugar speculation, £35,000 in a hemp transaction and £50,000 in an iron venture. According to the *Morning Chronicle*, there were few outside the house of Rothschild who speculated to such an extent in foreign railways and mining undertakings.

Dickens also portrayed Jonas Chuzzlewit as both credulous and ignorant. He wrote, 'there is a simplicity of cunning no less than a simplicity of innocence'. This credulity extends to the victims of the Anglo-Bengalee Disinterested Loan and Life Assurance Company. Tigg Montague tells Jonas Chuzzlewit, 'I can tell you how many of 'em will buy annuities, effect insurances, bring us their money in a hundred shapes and ways, force it upon us, trust us as if we were the Mint, yet know no more about us than you do of that crossing sweeper at the corner'.

Great con men have an almost pathological capacity for self-delusion. During his first prison sentence, Ponzi wrote to his mother that he had a three-year contract as special assistant to the prison warden and that during that time he would not have to worry where his next meal or warm bed was coming from. Allen Stanford also fooled himself. In the early days of his bank, he reassured a friend that his property investments would pay off any debts. In early 2009, when his empire was being battered by the collapse of Madoff and the general financial crisis, he went to Las Vegas where he lost $515,000 gambling. He then flew to Tripoli, apparently under the impression that the Libyan government would rescue him. The head of the Libyan sovereign wealth fund was so unimpressed by Stanford that he withdrew some of Libya's existing investments. He then flew to Zurich looking for funds, but by then Alex Dalmady's critical article had been published so his chances of survival were almost nil.

Many of Madoff's investors seem to have had great faith in him; his friend Norman Levy died in 2005, aged 93. His last words to his children were 'Bernie Madoff, trust Bernie Madoff', and he appointed the great man as executor for his financial assets. If he is to be believed, Madoff shared that optimism. Looking back, it seems clear that what Madoff was doing was always questionable. As James Chanos pointed out, he broke all the basic rules: he did not produce any information about his investments; he said nothing about his business activities; and he produced no financial statements. As Chanos observed, if someone had come to him with a work of fiction about Madoff, he would have thrown it out as being too incredible. And yet people invested billions of dollars with him.

Elie Wiesel described how he was persuaded to buy into the Madoff dream. He had a friend who gave Wiesel a clever sales pitch; he said 'Look, you work so hard, what are you doing with your money?'

And Wiesel replied 'Look, we don't know – shares here and there'.

His friend then responded, 'It's true you are not rich enough, but I have a friend, and this friend is so great and so good'.

The man he was talking about was, of course, Bernie Madoff. Wiesel checked Madoff out, had dinner with him, discovered the names of some of the other people who were investing with him and eventually handed over all his money. Wiesel was justifiably angry and said that he was one of the greatest scoundrels, thieves, liars and criminals of recent years.

Great con men have three defining characteristics that set them apart from other people. First, as Elie Wiesel said, they can imagine things that the rest of us simply cannot imagine. Not only could Madoff and the others imagine their crimes, but they could also imagine that they could escape from the consequences of them. Second, they have the power to persuade others to buy into their dreams; what Ponzi and Madoff in particular were doing was simply unbelievable, but they were able to persuade others to invest their hard-earned money with them. But finally, what really distinguishes these men from the rest of humanity is that most of them seem to believe their own fantasies. Somehow they delude themselves, as well as their victims, that they have discovered the secret of acquiring unimaginable riches.

Sadly, Madoff will probably not be the last fraudster to deprive innocent victims of billions of pounds. Let us leave the last word to Dickens. In *Little Dorrit*, Ferdinand Barnacle, one of the minor characters, warns the hero Clennam that Merdle will not be the last fraudster to succeed, because there will always be greedy and naive people:

> 'My dear Mr Clennam,' returned Ferdinand, laughing, 'have you really such a verdant hope? The next man who has as large a capacity and as genuine a taste for swindling, will succeed as well. Pardon me, but I think you really have no idea how the human bees will swarm to the beating of any old tin kettle; in that fact lies the complete manual of governing them. When they can be got to believe that the kettle is made of the precious metals, in that fact lies the whole power of men like our late lamented. No doubt there are here and there,' said Ferdinand politely, 'exceptional cases, where people have been taken in for what appeared to them to be much better reasons; and I need not go far to find such a case; but they don't invalidate the rule. Good day! I hope that when I have the pleasure of seeing you, next, this passing cloud will have given place to sunshine. Don't come a step beyond the door. I know the way out perfectly. Good day!'

Chapter Two

The Document Forgers

Fooling people gave me a sense of power and superiority. I believe this is what led to my forging activities

Forgery has always been with us – everything from paintings to wine has been forged since the earliest times. When he was a young man, Michelangelo made a life-size sculpture of Cupid. Lorenzi di Pierfrancesco di Medici advised him to make it appear like an ancient piece of work and send it to Rome, where it would sell for a good price. In one version of the story, Michelangelo did change the appearance of his Cupid to make it look ancient; in another, Baldassare de Milanese bought it and buried it in his vineyard. He then dug it up and sold it as a classical piece.

Some scholars and art forgers believe that Michelangelo's Cupid still survives. In 1995 one professor claimed to have recognized it at the French Cultural Delegation in New York and it became known as the Fifth Avenue Cupid. However, another claimed that this was a forgery created around 1900 to look like a damaged Michelangelo. Cupids buried in vineyards, modern copies of slightly suspect Michelangelo sculptures – welcome to the world of fakes and forgeries!

In this chapter we will look at what constitutes forgery, what sorts of forgeries are found in libraries and archives, forgery as a joke and as an illegal activity. We will also look at some examples from the eighteenth and nineteenth centuries and consider the motives of forgers and their victims. We will scrutinize the role of 'experts' and the ways in which forgery can be detected, using three case studies: the Himmler forger; Mark Hofmann and the Emily Dickinson poem; and the two British forgers, Wise and Foreman.

Some historical documents once considered forgeries have subsequently been rehabilitated and we will examine them, as well as considering the impact of forgery in the past and its future in the digital world. The forgers we will meet along the way will illustrate the main behaviours and the full range of character types typical of such people – the hardboiled, the sad, the delusional and the violent.

An examination of forgery is important because, as we will see, forgers, like sturdy beggars, begging letter writers and con men, are essentially trying to cheat people. They have much in common with the other rogues we are considering and their motives are similar, usually either gain, but sometimes glory or even just a simple delight in tricking people. It is tempting to see forgers as isolated figures, sitting in basements surrounded by paper, ink and mysterious chemicals. In fact, successful forgers are tricksters and they have to possess extensive knowledge of the psychology of their victims and how to exploit their weaknesses. Their technical skills need to be combined with a great deal of human understanding and it is by looking at these personal aspects of their work that we gain a greater insight into how the whole psychological process of cheating works.

Forgery and begging have a long and close connection. Henry Mayhew, the journalist and social researcher, told the story of Alexander Fyfe, who hired a writer to produce an elaborate document setting out his financial problems. These were apparently caused when his son-in-law absconded, leaving Fyfe owing a large amount of money. The writer also produced a subscription list giving the names of people who had already made donations to help Fyfe, including clergymen, aldermen, senior army officers and companies. Fyfe could use the documents to prove his credibility with other potential donors.

Fyfe's writer was part of a long tradition. From the sixteenth century individuals made money by providing fake documents to back up the claims of beggars. In the earliest works, they are referred to as 'Jarckmen' or 'Patricos' and they produced licences to beg for alms for hospitals or for people who wished to pretend that they were ship-wrecked sailors or that their houses had been burned down.

It is worth spending a little time trying to define exactly what a forgery is. There is a whole spectrum of activities covering different ways of creating copies of other people's work. At one extreme is counterfeiting – making exact copies of something that already exists. A fake £5 note would be an example of counterfeiting. Next on the spectrum comes forgery, which involves creating something similar to an existing artefact but which has no exact real parallel. A £6 note would be a forgery.

Finally comes plagiarism – passing off your own work as somebody else's. Attitudes to plagiarism have varied over the years; many writers have borrowed material from others and at some dates this was more acceptable. As is well-known, Shakespeare 'borrowed' from Holinshed's *Chronicles*, Chapman's translation of *Homer*, North's *Plutarch*, among other sources. The Tudor writer of rogue literature, Robert Greene, regarded this as unacceptable and called Shakespeare an 'upstart crow beautified with our feathers'. Ironically, Greene was himself committing a form of plagiarism by saying this, since the up-start crow is a reference to Aesop's fable about a crow which disguised itself with peacock's feathers.

There are three types of forgery commonly found in archives and libraries. The first is the alteration of registers and other documents, while the second is the recreation of an existing document. Examples include the Texas forgers, who made printed copies of rare Texas handbills, and Mark Hofmann, who made an original manuscript of a Daniel Boone letter previously only known in a printed version. The most dangerous form of document forgery is the total fabrication – Hofmann's fantasies about the origins of Mormonism or The National Archives' own forger, who believed that Churchill had Himmler murdered.

Some forgeries are simply malicious, without any reference to anything in the real world. The Protocols of the Elders of Zion – the alleged proof of a Jewish and Masonic conspiracy to achieve world domination – provide an example of this. It is believed that they were forged in Russia in 1902 or 1903. They are only known from printed copies, as no original manuscript has come to light. Two witnesses said they had seen a French manuscript claimed to be the original of the protocols. Both had serious doubts about the genuineness of this document and one, Princess Catherine Radziwill, later suggested that the protocols were created on the instructions of the head of the Russian secret service in Paris. But it is now widely accepted that there were no protocols, no elders and no manuscripts.

While the motivation behind the protocols forgery was clearly malign, the distinction between forgery as a crime and forgery as either literature or even a private joke is not always wholly clear. Some writers have used forgery-like techniques to add verisimilitude to a story. Two of Daniel Defoe's works, *Robinson Crusoe* and *A Journal of the Plague Year*, mix fiction with accounts of real events. John Payne Collier, the great Shakespeare forger, said that one of the saddest days of his early life was when he discovered that the whole story of Robinson Crusoe was invention and not reality. George Steevens, the eighteenth century Shakespeare editor, spent many years producing forgeries – including the tombstone of Hardicanute – as practical, if malicious, jokes on his friends and enemies. Even the great Argentinean writer Jorge Luis Borges was not above passing off his works of fiction as translations from obscure foreign texts.

The horror writer H.P. Lovecraft liked to hint at knowledge to which humans should not have access. In his writing, he often mentioned books containing such knowledge, including a purely invented work called the *Necronomicon*. He refers to this text in a number of his stories, always referring to it as the frightful or dreaded *Necronomicon*, and occasionally quotes passages from it. These frequent references to the book planted the belief in a real evil tome in the minds of his readers.

In 1927 Lovecraft wrote a fictional history of the book, which was published after his death. He said that the manuscript was originally written in Damascus by the half-crazed Arab, Abdul Alhazred, shortly before his death in 738 (he was apparently seized by a monster in broad daylight before terrified witnesses). The original title of the book was *Al Azif*, supposedly the nocturnal noise made by insects, which sounds like the howling of demons. The book was later translated into Greek in 950, when it got its modern name. Lovecraft claimed that some readers of the book made terrible experiments and it was banned by Patriarch Michael in 1050. A Latin translation was made in 1228 and both the Latin and Greek versions were banned by Pope Gregory IX in 1232. Later editions were published in Germany, Spain and Italy and the English magician Dr John Dee translated it, but only fragments of his work survive. Copies were supposed to exist in the National Library of France, the British Library, Widener Library at Harvard University, the University of Buenos Aires and Miskatonic University, Arkham, Massachusetts.

So, a book that never existed gained a degree of veracity because Lovecraft associated it with real people – Patriarch Michael, Pope Gregory IX and Dr John Dee. Some readers were taken in. There are stories about people approaching booksellers and librarians asking for copies, as well as phony references added to library card catalogues. Indeed there have been at least four published 'texts' of the *Necronomicon*, starting with a version in the late 1970s edited by a person called 'Simon', which is based on Sumerian mythology with references to Lovecraft and Aleister Crowley. In 1978 there was a 'translation' of a cipher text by Dr John Dee, with an introduction by the writer Colin Wilson, as well as a fictional account by Donald Tyson in 2004. The most extraordinary text, however was a 1973 version written in an indecipherable, mysterious language known as 'Duriac.' Even stranger is the suggestion by the British occult writer Kenneth Grant that the *Necronomicon* exists as an astral book, which can be accessed through ritual magic or dreams. This is about as obscure as forgery gets.

Forgery was not regarded by the law as a serious matter until 1563, when parliament laid down that convicted forgers should have their ears cut off and their noses slit. But it was in the eighteenth century that the crime began to come into its own. This was because from the end of the seventeenth century the economy was in transition from reliance on cash to dependence on paper transactions. According to

Dr Johnson, 'The greater part of all moveable property is now wandering in bills, round land and sea and stands wholly upon the faith of paper. If this faith should by frequent and successful forgery become suspicious and uncertain, the traffic of mankind must stop and the wealth of thousands be annihilated'.

Thirty-six statutes passed in the eighteenth century made forgery of various different types of documents criminal offences. Forging stamp duty records, land transfers, wills, seamen's tickets and even state lottery tickets could get people sent to Tyburn. Between 1750 and 1794 there were two or three executions of forgers in London every year. Forgers were less likely to be reprieved than any other sort of criminal aside from murderers and, according to the penal reformer, John Howard, 71 out of 95 convicted forgers were hanged between 1749 and 1771.

The forging of seamen's wills was very common. Criminals would go to the Navy Pay Office and find the names of sailors who had died at sea and whose back pay had not been claimed by relatives. They would then go to Doctors' Commons, near St Paul's Cathedral, to visit the Prerogative Court of Canterbury. The court was responsible for administering the probate of people who had died overseas and here they would submit a forged will. The amounts claimed could be substantial, particularly if the sailor had been at sea for a number of years or if he was entitled to prize money. William Richardson was sent to Tyburn in 1765 for forging the will of John Steward, a mariner on HMS *Epreuve*. Richardson was a waterman by trade and had been involved in at least four other cases where wills or related documents concerning sailors had been forged.

The most famous forger to be hanged was Dr William Dodd, a well-known preacher and promoter of good causes. Notorious for his extravagant lifestyle, he was nicknamed the 'Macaroni Parson' because at that time, a 'macaroni' was a popular term for a man who dressed in an elaborate and affected way. The word probably originated with rich young men who went to Italy on the Grand Tour and developed a taste for pasta and fashionable clothes. Despite winning £1,000 in a lottery, Dodd was always short of cash and he tried to bribe the wife of the Lord Chancellor to have him appointed to the lucrative post of Rector of St George's Hanover Square. This failed and he was stripped of his other posts, becoming an object of public ridicule.

Desperate for money, Dodd forged a bond in the name of his former pupil, the Earl of Chesterfield, and was arrested, tried and sentenced to death. There was a campaign to secure a pardon for him. Dr Johnson wrote speeches, petitions and letters in his defence and allowed Dodd to pass off a sermon he had written, 'The Convict's Address' as his own work. When asked if Dodd could have written it, given the stress he was under, Johnson made his famous remark 'Depend upon it sir, when a man knows he is to be hanged in a fortnight, it concentrates his mind wonderfully'. However, Johnson's sermon made no difference and Dodd took his final trip to Tyburn on 27 June 1777.

The eighteenth century was also a period when people became interested in antiquarian matters and collected coins, medals and historical objects. The Society of Antiquaries dates from 1718 and the British Museum was established in 1753. Satirists believed that antiquaries were gullible victims of rogues and forgers and described how they would acquire such things as 'Pontius Pilate's Wife's Chambermaid's Sister's Hat' and 'Falstaff's Corkscrew'.

Georgian England saw a huge growth of interest in literature and literary criticism. With it came a new industry of forging plays and inventing poets, whose masters were James Macpherson and Thomas Chatterton. Macpherson produced two collections of poetry, which he claimed were translations from ancient Gaelic verses. The authenticity of these was immediately challenged, mainly because of his failure to produce the original manuscripts.

Dr Johnson was a particularly harsh critic, insisting that there could be no proof unless the original manuscripts were made available. He said that it was like a court case in which somebody was trying to prove that a particular man was alive: 'You aver he is alive and you bring fifty men to prove it. I answer "Why do you not produce the man?"' Johnson also had doubts about the quality of the poetry. When asked whether any man today could write such poetry, Johnson replied, 'Yes. Many men. Many women. And many children'. Nevertheless, many people were believers in Macpherson and visitors to the Highlands and Islands claimed to have met men who said they had known the Gaelic versions of his work since they were children.

Thomas Chatterton was a stranger, more tragic figure. Born in Bristol in 1752, he became obsessed by the Middle Ages and adopted the persona of a fictitious fifteenth century monk, Thomas Rowley, in whose name he produced poems that he claimed to be translations of old manuscripts he had found in the Church of St Mary Redcliffe, and subsequently sold to local newspapers. At the age of 17 Chatterton decided to seek his fortune in London, where he made small amounts of money selling satirical verse and prose. However, his earnings were tiny and within a few months he committed suicide.

Chatterton achieved a degree of posthumous fame with the publication of an edition of his poems entitled *Poems supposed to have been written at Bristol by Thomas Rowley and others, in the Fifteenth Century.* Within a year or so, the truth behind his work was recognized, although there were still people willing to defend him. The story of this young man dying alone in an attic in Holborn touched the hearts of the romantic poets and indeed, it seems to have been a sort of badge of honour amongst them to have written a tribute. Keats, Shelley, Coleridge and Wordsworth all had a go and Wordsworth's description of him as 'the marvellous boy' is Chatterton's best-known epitaph.

Why do people commit forgery? At first sight, their motives appear simple – they want to make money or enhance their prestige. Mark Hofmann sold his Mormon forgeries to collectors and the Church of Latter Day Saints for large sums. John Drewe made money by forging papers, which he inserted into the Tate Gallery and other archives to establish the provenance of paintings faked by his accomplice, John Myatt. Clive Driver tampered with catalogues and deaccession records at the Rosenbach Museum and Library to cover up his thefts. Lee Israel, broke and living in a miserable apartment, reportedly began her life of crime to fund some veterinary treatment for her kitten.

Others wanted to make a political or historical point. In the 1930s, William Franklin Horn published manuscripts on genealogy and the history of Washington County, Pennsylvania, apparently designed to dramatize the lives of the pioneers of western Pennsylvania, some of whom may have been his ancestors. The creator of the Himmler forgeries wanted to suggest that Winston Churchill was behind the death of this leading Nazi.

Others had more complex motives. William-Henry Ireland, born in 1775, was the illegitimate son of his father's housekeeper. Ireland forged Shakespeare manuscripts and plays, hoping to win the goodwill of his father, the publisher Samuel Ireland, who regarded him with indifference. He was fascinated by the life and death of Thomas Chatterton and almost certainly knew the works of James Macpherson.

Let us dig a little deeper into the motives of those who forged for money. Hofmann certainly made significant sums by selling forgeries to the Church of Latter Day Saints. He was born a Mormon, but lost his faith and he claimed to have forged documents that were consistent with Mormon history as he perceived it. At the heart of the Mormon faith is the Book of Mormon, a translation of a book of gold plates revealed by the Angel Moroni to Joseph Smith, the founder of the Church. One of the earliest works of anti-Mormon propaganda, *Mormonism Unveiled* (1834), criticized Smith for being involved in folk magic and using magical methods to search for buried treasure. Indeed Smith had been prosecuted in 1826 for scrying (using a crystal ball or similar object to discover hidden knowledge), then an offence under the New York penal code.

Hofmann forged documents confirming the allegations, including a letter from Joseph Smith to Joseph Stowell with instructions for using a split hazel rod to find treasure. Worse still was the notorious Salamander letter, in which a white salamander, not the Angel Moroni, showed Smith the gold plates. (Salamanders are traditionally associated with folk magic.)

Later, Hofmann moved away from forging Mormon documents and turned to producing papers relating to early American history. His final collection of forgeries returns to Mormon history – he claimed to have access to the 'McLellin collection' – a supposedly extensive group of documents written by William E. McLellin, an early Mormon apostle who eventually broke with the Church of Latter Day Saints. Hofmann did not have time to forge a sufficiently large collection of documents and, in an effort to distract attention, he began to make bombs. He killed Steven Christensen, a local document collector and Kathy Sheets, the wife of Christensen's former employer. A third bomb exploded in Hofmann's own car, damaging his hand. During the subsequent police investigation, conclusive evidence of his forgery was found. He pleaded guilty to second degree murder and forgery and was sentenced to life imprisonment.

John Payne Collier was a serious Victorian Shakespeare scholar, who had no need to be a forger, since he had made some genuine discoveries. Had he stuck to legitimate scholarship, Collier would have found a place in the canon of Shakespearian scholars as a hero, not a villain. Sadly, from his earliest major work, the *History of English Dramatic Poetry*, he invented new documents or amended existing ones. His major work was the so-called *Perkins Folio*, a Second Folio of Shakespeare heavily annotated by an 'Old Corrector'. The annotations included changes to spellings, the omission of parts of scenes and stage directions.

Collier was eventually unmasked by the scholarship of Sir Frederic Madden of the British Museum, and the solicitor C.M. Ingleby. Collier has had his defenders, among them Dewey Ganzel in his 1982 study *Fortune and Men's Eyes*. Ganzel claims that Collier was the victim of class bias – a hard-working lower-class boy attacked by upper class dilettantes. Yet, a recent and definitive study of Collier by Arthur Freeman and Janet Ing Freeman finds for the prosecution. Writing in his diary in 1882, the aged Collier confessed, 'I am bitterly sad and most sincerely grieved that in every way I am such a despicable offender ... I am ashamed of almost every act of my life ... My repentance is bitter and sincere'.

E.K. Chambers has described Collier's behaviour as one of 'a few cases where neither controversial fervour, nor greed for lucre, nor the spirit of mischief provides an adequate explanation'. He put it down to some 'little twist of the brain' or 'some strange freak of temperament'. However, Chambers' view is too simplistic and something else also seems to have been going on.

What that something might have been becomes clearer in the case of John Drewe. Born John Cockett in 1948, little is known about his early life. He dropped out of school and got a job at the UK Atomic Energy Authority. Later he lived with an Israeli expatriate, Bat-Sheva Goudsmid. From 1985, he made money by forging papers, which he inserted into the Tate Gallery and other archives, to verify the provenance of paintings faked by his accomplice, John Myatt. In 1995, after Drewe left Goudsmid, she found incriminating papers he had left behind and reported him to the police. Drewe's accomplice also testified against him. In 1999 he was tried, convicted and sentenced to six years' imprisonment. Drewe maintained his innocence throughout the trial and subsequently.

At the trial, the prosecuting counsel said the effort he put into the deception suggested 'an intellectual delight in fooling people and contempt for experts'. Drewe seems to have been having fun at the art world's expense. He gave the Tate £20,000 to help catalogue the archives and offered to give the gallery two (forged) Bissière paintings. Fortunately, they were not of a suitable quality and the Tate turned them down.

It is this need to demonstrate their skill, coupled with contempt for the expert, that marks the true forger of genius. Writing in *The New York Times*, Peter Landesman declared:

A forger's chief motivation is typically intellectual gamesmanship. Embittered by the spurning of his own work, he takes satisfaction in suckering the entire art world en masse, then pulling aside the curtain, exposing himself as a renegade genius and the art experts as the frauds and fools.

This motivation is very similar to that of many internet hackers today, who enjoy showing their friends just how clever they are.

Mark Hofmann also had a slightly murky past. As a young man, Mark had been interested in electroplating and managed to produce a copy of a rare coin. He sent the coin to the US Treasury Department, which authenticated it. Mark described how he felt when he took his forged Anthon transcript to church officials. 'There was, of course, a little bit of fear involved since, of course, it was a forged document. There was some excitement involved, a feeling of duping them'. He developed this theme in a letter to his parole board: 'As far back as I can remember, I have liked to impress people through my deceptions. In fact, some of my earliest memories are of doing magic and card tricks. Fooling people gave me a sense of power and superiority. I believe this is what led to my forging activities'.

This motivation was best described 300 years ago by the great classical scholar and royal librarian, Richard Bentley in his exposure of the forged epistles of Phalaris. He described the motives of a forger as either simple gain or 'glory and affectation as an exercise of style and an ostentation of wit ... to speak freely the greatest part of mankind are so easily imposed on in this way, that there is too great an invitation to put the trick on them'.

All forgers need people who are willing to buy into the false world they create. The motives of the customer may be simply the desire of a collector to possess – 'randy for antique' in Philip Larkin's phrase. Jenkins Garrett, an inadvertent buyer of a forged Texas broadsheet, best describes the inner world of the collector:

It must be recognised that when a rare item is offered to a collector which is considered 'a pearl of great price', the normal defences tend to fail and the primary force which takes over is the desire to close the purchase quickly before the item is offered to another collector.

Garrett had bought one of a series of forged handbills and other rare printed documents created in the 1960s and early 1970s, intended for sale to rich collectors and the increasingly wealthy universities in the western United States. Curiously, the forger, who was never prosecuted, always claimed that he was not planning a fraud, simply intending to produce facsimile packs of significant Texas documents. Some victims had slightly more generous motives: a number of Mormons who bought Hofmann's finest works subsequently donated them to the Church of Latter Day Saints. Others were driven by a desire for knowledge.

In the eighteenth century, there was a huge interest in the life of William Shakespeare. However, writing a biography of Shakespeare is difficult because apart from his will, there is very little personal material available – there are no plays in his handwriting and no letters. The only specimens of his handwriting are the signatures on the will and on a couple of other formal records.

To write a biography of Shakespeare, you need to rely mainly on legal and tax records and a range of formal and not terribly exciting sources. But people wanted more and forgers were around to supply them. John Byng, the diarist, described how he bought a crossbar from a chair that had once belonged to Shakespeare.

The forger William-Henry Ireland provided a whole range of exciting new Shakespeare documents, including letters to Anne Hathaway and Elizabeth I, as well as original manuscripts of *Hamlet* and *King Lear*. Many people were fooled; Ireland's most famous victim was James Boswell, the biographer of Dr Johnson. In 1795 Boswell stood in front of the 'original' manuscript of *King Lear*, knelt down on the floor and kissed it and said 'I shall now die contented since I have lived to see this present day'. Ireland's downfall was dramatic; the first production of his new 'Shakespeare' play, *Vortigern and Rowena*, was booed off the stage, two days after Edmund Malone, the greatest Shakespeare scholar of the age, had published a 400-page exposé of Ireland's earlier forged manuscripts.

Above all, forgers rely on the willingness of customers to suspend disbelief. According to Rick Grunder, a rare documents dealer who specialized in Mormon manuscripts, Hofmann 'convinced us that he knew something we did not, that he had access to things we could otherwise never hope to find ... He was the Mormon Indiana Jones who could lead us to impossible treasures of information and wealth'. Clearly, good acting skills, as well as technical forging skills are essential for a successful forger.

If forgery is suspected, then expert advice is needed. However, it is important to get two opinions because, unfortunately, the most obvious expert may also be the forger. Anyone seeking to authenticate a pamphlet by Swinburne, Browning or Ruskin in 1920 would have gone to Thomas J. Wise, doyen of collectors and bibliographer of those writers and, as we will see, the leading forger of their works. One American gallery owner was worried about a Giacometti he had acquired for £105,000 and turned to a firm of experts, Art Research Associates, for advice. The proprietor of the firm met the owner at the National Art Library and showed him catalogues and invoices tracing the picture's path out of Giacometti's studio. The dealer was convinced. But the company was run by John Drewe, who charged the man $600 to use evidence Drewe had concocted himself to authenticate a painting that he had faked in the first place.

Sometimes experts are not criminal, just mistaken. When a Mr Evans showed Frederic Madden of the British Museum the notorious 'bellows portrait' of Shakespeare by P.H. Zincke, a forgery already exposed by Abraham Wivell 30 years before, Madden expressed his views in his diary 'What an ass this Mr Evans must be, to buy a portrait of such a character after the fraud had been detected and exposed so publicly! Verily the number of fools is infinite'. His views were echoed nearly two centuries later by the twentieth century forger Lee Israel, who believed that most dealers didn't know that 'provenance was not the capital of Rhode Island'.

Some people just do not seem able to help themselves. In 1983, Phillip Knightley wrote to his bosses reminding them that in 1968, the Thomson Organisation, then owners of *The Sunday Times*, had paid a large sum of money to a Polish arms dealer for the 'Mussolini Diaries'. It turned out that the diaries were written by an Italian woman, Anna Panvini and her 84-year-old mother. Nothing daunted, the next owner of *The Sunday Times* bought the 'Hitler Diaries'.

Hugh Trevor Roper achieved fame in the 1970s, when he wrote a biography of Sir Edmund Backhouse, who lived in Beijing from 1899 to 1944 and worked as a scholar, translator, fixer, arms dealer and spy. Trevor Roper claimed that Backhouse's memoirs, in which Backhouse claimed that he had an affair with Oscar Wilde and acted opposite Sarah Bernhardt, were largely imaginary. He then destroyed his reputation in the 1980s by authenticating the Hitler Diaries.

* * *

At Hofmann's preliminary trial in 1987, the former director of libraries and archives for the Church of Latter Day Saints testified that Mormon leaders accepted Hofmann's documents without question, after he had provided affidavits regarding the provenance of his first two major acquisitions. Forensic tests had been few, but Mormon historians had checked the documents for accuracy. The director of special collections at Utah University said, 'I buy a lot of things from Sam Weller [the well-known Salt Lake City bookseller], for instance, but Sam rarely tells me where he gets things'.

At his parole hearing, Victoria Palacios, a board member said 'I can't believe people didn't catch on'.

Hofmann replied 'I'm sure neither can they. Neither can I'.

While some experts failed to check the provenance of documents sufficiently, others found it difficult to accept that they had been conned even in the face of strong evidence. A dealer who bought one of Drewe's fake Giacomettis continued to maintain that it was one of the best examples of the artist's work that he had seen.

One crucial weapon in defeating the forger is information. In 1955, there were only two known copies of the printed broadside of William Barrett Travis's 'Victory or Death' letter from the Alamo. Another copy surfaced in 1972 and was sold in New York. In the next 13 years, at least 11 more copies were sold. No doubt their buyers thought they were getting a rarity, but might have been less sanguine had they known about the large number of copies available. One of the benefits of the internet is that it increases knowledge and consequently reduces the sphere in which a forger can operate.

Documents have four aspects: physicality; provenance; appearance; and content. In investigating suspect documents, each of these aspects needs to be considered, since none alone can necessarily prove or disprove the authenticity of a document. Too much exposure to detective fiction gives a biased and exaggerated view of the power of forensic science. It is easy to see the world of detecting forgeries as something out of Conan Doyle; particularly those classic works by Sherlock Holmes, *On the Typewriter and Its Relation to Crime* and *Upon the Dating of Old Documents*. In fact, while scientific evidence can help identify fraud, it is no more valuable than expertise about content or provenance.

Collier was unmasked, in part, because traces of pencil guidelines were observed on some of the documents he forged. Hofmann was relatively well-read in the field of manuscripts, having studied *Great Forgers and Famous Fakes*, as well as books on making ink. Clifford Irving is famous for producing a faked 'autobiography' of Howard Hughes, but he first studied the subject in great detail when he wrote a biography of the Hungarian art forger Elmyr de Hory (filmed by Orson Welles as *Fake*).

Hofmann took great care to create appropriate materials for his works. He studied calligraphy and made his own ink from beeswax, carbon and linseed oil, burning seventeenth century paper to make the carbon because he feared carbon dating of the ink would reveal that it was new. John Myatt, who forged paintings for John Drewe, was much more casual; he used a mixture of emulsion paint and K-Y Gel as a fast-drying substitute for oil paints.

A good example of the use of physical evidence comes from W. Thomas Taylor, who spent a lot of time identifying forgeries of early Texas printed documents, such as the Texas Declaration of Independence. The owner of a printing business, he was sensitive to issues of typography. An 1835 handbill announcing a horse race in Columbia looked odd to him and the type did not match anything the alleged printer F.C. Gray had used. Eventually, the type was identified by a member of Taylor's staff as Century – a design not introduced until 1896.

On its own, forensic science is not enough. Charles Hamilton, a well-known expert and the author of *Great Forgers and Famous Fakes*, authenticated one of Hofmann's forgeries, while a paper specialist, an ink specialist and a rare books dealer found no reason to believe that the Salamander letter was not genuine. George Throckmorton, an expert document examiner involved in detecting forgeries who worked on the Hofmann case, explained some of the issues:

> You can say that gallotannate ink is consistent with ink used in the nineteenth century, but it could also have been made yesterday in the bathroom sink. You can say that paper is consistent with nineteenth-century paper; but if you avoid whiteners or other recent additions to the stock, you can buy rag paper today that's just the same. Besides it might not be that hard to get old paper. You could steal it from books published at the right time, or whatever.

Provenance is also crucial in determining the authenticity of documents. Mark Hofmann went to elaborate lengths to authenticate the Anthon Transcript, the contemporary transcript of the golden plates unearthed by Joseph Smith following a visit from the Angel Moroni. He showed A.J. Simmonds, head of special collections at Utah University, a Bible into which a mysterious letter had been glued. After much labour, they removed the letter and found it to be the Anthon

Transcript. A well-known Mormon scholar authenticated it. Questions then arose as to where Hofmann had obtained the Bible. He said a friend, Ansel White, had bought it at a sale in the Midwest. But where and who from? Hofmann then found an antiques dealer, Dorothy Dean, who showed him her sales record. One item did not have a purchase next to it and Hofmann persuaded her that this mysterious item was clearly the sale of the Bible to Mr White and she signed an affidavit to that effect.

Hofmann also tried hard to provide a provenance for his 'Oath of a Freeman', America's first printed document. He took a copy of a patriotic ballad written for Abraham Lincoln's re-election in 1864, photographed it, removed the heading and substituted the title 'Oath of a Freeman'. He then rephotographed it and printed it. Next he took this new 'Oath of a Freeman' to the Argosy Book Store in New York and put it in one of their boxes of ephemera. He then 'discovered' it and bought it. The Argosy Book Store gave him a genuine invoice for the document and he could point to this when people asked about the provenance of his forged 'Oath of a Freeman'. 'I found it in the ephemera box at Argosy Book Store and here's their invoice'.

The nineteenth century French forger Denis Vrain-Lucas created letters written between famous people who had never corresponded. He was caught out when he wrote some letters between Blaise Pascal and Isaac Newton. Unkind critics pointed out that Newton was only 12 at the time of this correspondence. Nothing daunted, Vrain-Lucas indulged in a little retrospective authentication by forging a letter from Newton's tutor confirming that he had corresponded with Pascal.

Other forgers relied on altering or adding to existing archives. Collier, the Shakespeare forger, had access to the collections at Devonshire House, Bridgewater House and Dulwich College, which he polluted with forgeries. Among those forgers who added material to archives, the nineteenth century record agent Herbert Davies was perhaps the most blatant. He was hired by Lieutenant-Colonel Robert Shipway of Grove House Chiswick to write his family tree. He decided to take the easy way out by forging the evidence.

W.P.W. Phillimore, the pioneering genealogist and records editor, spent a lot of time and effort uncovering Davies's activities. Phillimore described how he visited the vicar at Stonehouse, Gloucestershire, who kept a parish register. Phillimore said that he had no opportunity of seeing the register, but the vicar informed him that after 'Dr' Davies's visit an entry appeared to have become much more legible. When Phillimore challenged Davies about this, he explained that he had breathed upon it and that the carbonic acid in his breath affected the faded writing, adding that a mixture containing carbonic acid was used for this purpose at the British Museum.

Among Davies's more unusual exploits was borrowing a hammer and chisel from a blacksmith in Mangotsfield so that he could sneak up, to the belfry and carve an entirely false inscription on a beam, recording the donation of a bell by a member of the Shipway family. He also had a coffin dug up and used acid to alter the inscription on the coffin plate, providing another link in the family tree. Lieutenant-Colonel Shipway was the son of a tailor and ran a breeches-making business, but he had ambitions to rise in society and he paid £683 to Davies to provide him with a pedigree so he could acquire a coat of arms. During Davies's trial, the press ridiculed Shipway for his snobbery and gullibility. The first piece of 'evidence' Davies had given him was his grandfather's watch, hallmarked 1782 but inscribed 1762. Davies pleaded guilty to forgery and was sent down for three years.

Some forgers were even less subtle. William Henry Ireland first told his father that during a dinner he had met a wealthy gentleman in possession of many old papers which had been in his family for a century and a half and were possibly of interest to the young William Henry. Ireland had then visited the wealthy gentleman's chambers and was shown a chest containing many old manuscripts, in which he found the Shakespeare material. Later he began referring to the man as Mr H. and to claim that he had further treasures at his country house. Eventually, William Henry's father Samuel wrote a series of letters to 'Mr H.' A bizarre situation developed in which Samuel was writing letters to the fictitious gentleman and William Henry was replying.

Appearance can help alert curators to the possibility of fraud. One of the defining features of the Texas forgeries was that they looked too clean, having no annotations showing previous owners. Old-fashioned connoisseurship – the ability to sense that something is wrong with a document or object – is one of the best weapons to protect collecting institutions against forgers.

One of the few people to have recognized a Hofmann forgery was Randy Wilson, a Salt Lake City collector, who persuaded Hofmann to refund the purchase price of a pirated copy of *The Latter Day Saints Emigrants Guide*. H. Ross Perot, billionaire and presidential candidate, had a similar sense about a Texas forgery. He was offered a *Victory or*

Death broadsheet, but would not buy it until Don Etherington, a conservator at the University of Texas, had taken it to Yale and compared it with a genuine copy there. He found a misformed letter 'a' in the word *flag* – something that could not happen with metal type. Perot returned the document to the dealer.

The content of a document is essential in proving its authenticity. Do the facts stack up? Is the date, the spelling and the use of language appropriate? Gerald and Sandra Tanner cast doubt on the Salamander letter because its content was too similar to E.D. Howe's 1834 work *Mormonism Unveiled*.

The Himmler Forgeries, which purported to show that Himmler had been assassinated on the orders of the British Government, were first noticed by the German historian, Ernst Haiger. He was particularly concerned about a letter from Hugh Dalton, the Minister of Economic Warfare, to Anthony Eden, Foreign Secretary, dated 28 February 1941. Almost everything about this letter is wrong. It is addressed to Mr A. Eden, Foreign Office; whereas the correct title would have been 'The Right Honourable Anthony Eden, MC'. Dalton addressed his fellow minister as 'Dear Minister', rather than 'Dear Eden' or 'Dear Foreign Secretary'. The crucial piece of evidence is Dalton's mention of a meeting he and Eden had had with the Prime Minister 'yesterday'. He went on to suggest a further meeting on the following Saturday. This was impossible, since Eden had left the country on 12 February for a visit to Egypt, Turkey and Greece and did not return until 10 April.

A similar historical error showed one of Collier's discoveries to be a forgery. He printed a petition from the Lord Chamberlain's Players in his *History of English Dramatic Poetry* (1831). This was part of a planning dispute in 1596 with residents in the Blackfriars area of London, who did not want the noise and inconvenience of a new theatre. The document is the first reference to Shakespeare as a player and is signed by him, as well as Burbage, Heming, Kempe and Sly. It contains a bit of elaboration 'in the summer season your Petitioners are able to play at their new built house on the Bankside called the Globe'. At the time of publication, nobody suspected this document, as it seemed genuine and the reference to the Globe fitted in with accepted opinion that it had been built in 1594. It was not until 1874 that J.O. Halliwell showed that the Globe could not have been built before December 1598, so, clearly the whole petition must be a fake.

Identification of forgeries often requires consideration of every aspect of a document. This is exemplified by five of the Himmler Forgeries at the UK National Archives. Initially, the attention of staff at the archives had been drawn to some suspect documents relating to an alleged plot to murder Himmler. The staff checked a range of related documents and found three messages in a Foreign Office file and two in War Office files which seemed suspicious. They noted the overall appearance of the documents and some strange use of language – the colloquialism 'he'd' and the American spelling 'defense', as well as the curious way the Duke of Windsor was referred to – 'Maj.-Gen HRH. The Duke of Windsor'. The documents were examined by the Forensic Science Service.

Forensic scientist Adam Craske reviewed the papers and found much to be concerned about. Microscopic examination showed that three letterheads on 'Ministry of Information' paper had been produced using fused black toner, probably from a laser printer. Careful inspection of the signatures showed that a pencil guideline had been produced to aid the creation of a forged signature. Traces of the pencil lines can still be seen on the paper.

In addition, comparison of the signature of Sir Robert Bruce-Lockhart, then head of the Political Warfare Executive, with other genuine examples showed that the signatures on the suspect documents were not authentic. Craske then found that they were all typed on similar paper, which was unlike any other paper in the three files in which the forgeries were found. The typeface and spacing of the typewriting on the five documents was similar too, and distinct from any other typewriting in the three files.

Ultimately, Craske concluded that there was strong evidence that all five questioned documents came from a single source – one typewriter, supply of paper, etc. He could not find any evidence of the date these forgeries were created. Yet, he felt that if, as is suggested by their content, they were supposed to have come from different sources, the links between them strongly supported the view that they were counterfeit.

At this point provenance became important. Two of the files had been transferred to The National Archives from the Ministry of Defence. The questionable documents were purported to be deciphered messages from The Hague and France, while another was a copy of a message to be sent in cipher to France. It was possible that they could have been typed by a clerk in the War Office. There was also a suspect

Foreign Office message sent from The Hague to London. However, it was unlikely that the same typewriter and paper would have been used to produce deciphers in the War Office and then to type a letter in the Foreign Office and archivists concluded that the documents were forged.

*   *   *

Lee Israel was a rather more sophisticated forger than the creator of the Himmler documents. Instead of using one typewriter, she had a collection of old machines which she used to create entertaining but fictitious letters from Noel Coward and Dorothy Parker. In her autobiography she described running down the road, hiding typewriters in waste bins, when the police were after her. She also stole some antique paper from a library and had letterheads printed on it. She used an upended television set as a light box to trace the signatures from stolen letters on to her forgeries.

One of Mark Hofmann's most remarkable forgeries was also a literary work: an Emily Dickinson poem. This came to light at a sale at Sotheby's in 1997. Hofmann had used the research of eminent Dickinson authority, Ralph Franklin, to produce an item capable of fooling any Dickinson expert, including Mr Franklin himself. Dickinson's handwriting changed considerably over her lifetime, and Hofmann used this information to produce a fake that was right for the period. Although he used contemporary paper, Hofmann did not have to fake the ink – the fake poem was written in pencil, which Dickinson used for all her writing except for final drafts.

While Franklin originally believed that the poem was genuine, he also noted that it read like a Hallmark Card rather than the work of a world-famous poet. The local library in Amherst, Massachusetts, where Emily Dickinson had lived, became very excited about this example of the work of their most famous resident and raised $24,000 to buy it at auction. Yet, as the sale was going through and a homecoming party was being planned for the poem, doubts began to surface. An attorney and document collector from Provo, Utah, Brent Ashworth, raised the alarm when he said that Hofmann had offered him a Dickinson poem and he thought it was the same one. Ashworth could speak with some authority, since he had spent hundreds of thousands of dollars buying faked material from Hofmann, and it is fairly certain that one of the bombs Hofmann made was intended to kill Ashworth.

The special collections librarian at Amherst, Daniel Lombardo, grew concerned that they had bought a fake. Careful examination of the manuscript yielded little useful data: the watermark seemed wrong and an example of the letter E showed signs of hesitation in writing. However, there was a lot more evidence pointing to the fact that the document was faked. In 1988 a list of forgeries had been found in Hofmann's prison cell, including a reference to Emily Dickinson. In 1990, a TV reporter from Salt Lake City had asked Hofmann whether the poem was a forgery and he had admitted it. Even so, Hofmann was known to have confessed to forgeries for which he had not been responsible.

The final piece in the jigsaw came when Lombardo discovered that the poem had been in the hands of the Gallery of History, a manuscript dealer in Las Vegas. Eventually, Lombardo contacted Shannon Flynn, who had acted as Hofmann's courier, and negotiated his business deals. Flynn admitted that, acting on behalf of Hofmann, he had delivered a poem by 'Emily Dickinson' to the Gallery of History in 1985.

*   *   *

Perhaps the most famous case of forgery detection to intrigue and entertain bibliographers for over 50 years was the case of Harry Buxton Forman and Thomas J. Wise. Both were self-made men who had made their own ways in the world. Forman was born in 1842, the son of a naval surgeon who lost all his money in a financial crash. He started working as a clerk in the Post Office and eventually rose to be second secretary, with responsibility for overseas mail. He was a failed poet and a distinguished editor of other people's work; his edition of the letters of Keats to Fanny Brawne was well-known, as was his publication of Shelley's poetry. He always had an interest in printing and typography – he produced different versions of his *Letters to Fanny Brawne* on large paper, coloured paper and vellum in order to increase sales to book collectors.

Thomas J. Wise spent his career with a company that dealt in and manufactured essential oils for use in perfumes and food flavouring and eventually rose to become a partner. He also occasionally used this company to sell some of his forgeries. Wise was a wealthy man; his estate was worth £138,000 when he died in 1937, decked in titles such as Honorary Fellow of Worcester College Oxford and President of the Bibliography Society.

Wise was even more dishonest than his partner Forman. In 1887 he became secretary of the Shelley Society and used its funds to produce an entire publication of his own and also used type set up and paid for by the society to print extra copies of their publications on coloured paper, which he sold for his own profit. His extravagance eventually bankrupted the society. He also bought damaged or defective copies of plays by Shakespeare and his contemporaries and later seventeenth century writers. He then 'improved' these by stealing replacements for the missing or damaged leaves from the British Museum.

Wise and Forman met in 1886 and soon produced a pirated edition of some Shelley poems copied from Edward Dowden's *Life of Shelley*. The pamphlet gave its place of publication as Philadelphia and it had a fake introduction, allegedly written by Charles Alfred Seymour of the Philadelphia Historical Society. In 1888 they produced a version of George Eliot's *Agatha*, an exact copy of the Shelley Society edition. From then until about 1900 they issued nearly a hundred pamphlets, which were all forgeries or pirated editions of the works of contemporary writers. They produced two types of forgeries: binary editions, which were simply fabrications of earlier editions, and creative forgeries, which pretended to be original imprints preceding previously known editions of an author's work. The most famous example of a creative forgery is their 1847 pamphlet of Elizabeth Barrett Browning's *Sonnets from the Portuguese*, dated three years earlier than the normally accepted first date of publication. Effectively they were creating first editions.

Forman and Wise were successful because authors were in the habit of publishing their shorter works as pamphlets limited to a few dozen copies, which they would give to their friends. Book collectors had developed an appetite for first editions in general and these privately printed limited editions in particular. Clearly there was money to be made. More importantly, there was not a huge risk of detection; the market in which Wise and Forman were operating was small and highly specialist and many of their victims lived in America.

Like all forgers of printed works and manuscripts, the major problem facing these two men was provenance and authenticity – how to explain the sudden appearance of hitherto unknown works and how to demonstrate that these were genuine. One way was to claim that they had made discoveries of forgotten batches of pamphlets and indeed Forman had made genuine discoveries, finding a number of copies of Browning's *Two Poems*. Wise claimed that in 1888 the publisher Ward Lock had cleared out some waste, including pamphlets which they regarded as of little account but he had recognized as interesting and valuable.

Then there were the mysterious suppliers. Wise claimed to have obtained material from F.G. Aylward, who worked for Thomas Carver, a Hereford book dealer, but in 1902, Wise claimed that Aylward had died a year before that. Hardly suspicious, but one of the investigators who did much to reveal the workings of the two forgers, Fannie Ratchford of Texas University, pointed out the disconcerting frequency with which Wise's sources died once they had served their purpose. How convenient to be able to point to a book dealer as the source of a pamphlet, only to regretfully announce that the dealer cannot supply further information since he passed away some time ago. When he was an old man, Wise was asked by two booksellers, John Carter and Graham Pollard, where he had obtained Browning's *Two Poems*. He said that it had turned up in the hands of Herbert George, a bookseller in the Goswell Road, London, around 1889. Scrupulous research has failed to identify Mr George.

However, the easiest thing to do was to use their positions as leading bibliographers to validate their own creations. Forman wrote *The Books of William Morris* (1897), which soon became the standard bibliography, but contained references to a number of his own forgeries. Wise and Forman both collaborated on *Literary Anecdotes of the Nineteenth Century*, which also mentioned material they had fabricated.

There was also the problem of distribution. The two forgers had to be careful; they did not want to release too many copies as this might push prices down or cause comment in the trade. At first, they were more tentative; Forman tended to swap his pamphlets for genuine works, while Wise sold his to private collectors and to book dealers. Wise had a particular victim, the American collector John Henry Wrenn. Wise sold him many forgeries and also real books at high prices. When the catalogue of Wrenn's library was published, nearly one in every five of the works described within it turned out to be forgeries. Wise was shameless in his treatment of Wrenn, playing him along. Yet, Wrenn's son said that his father's relationship with Wise was one of the richest and most satisfying of his life. From about 1897, Forman and Wise began to be less cautious and started to sell pamphlets at auctions in Britain and America. They may have realised that the game was nearly over and been trying to make as much money as they could while they had the opportunity.

Although the forgeries were not fully exposed until 1934, the shrewdest operators in the rare book trade always had deep suspicions of the two men. One of their earliest productions, Swinburne's *Siena*, was rapidly recognized as a forgery by *The Bookman* in 1892. Then, in 1897 Sydney Cockerell, one of William Morris's executors, wrote to Forman asking about a privately printed edition of *Pilgrims of Hope*, as well as editions of *God of the Poor* and *Sir Galahad*. Forman admitted to having published *Pilgrims of Hope*. Cockerell and F.S. Ellis, the other executor, hit back by placing an advertisement in *The Athenaeum* warning collectors of the existence of unauthorized reprints of Morris's work. They also informed the publishers of such material that they were engaging in an act of piracy and laying themselves open to proceedings under the Copyright Act.

A year later, the editors of *American Book Prices Current* warned about the many little privately printed pamphlets by celebrated modern authors being offered for sale from England and expressed the view that these pamphlets were manufactured. The writer had severe doubts about the claimed rarity of these pamphlets; he noted that Tennyson's *The Last Tournament* was described as a rare and valuable work, but as every Tennyson collector seemed to have acquired a copy recently, it could not be so rare nor so valuable.

In 1916 Charles Fairfax Murray came as close as he dared to outing the two forgers. He wrote to the son of an American collector about *Sir Galahad* by William Morris, which had been reprinted from the edition of 1858 by a speculator: 'it rests between two collectors of similar "rarities", either of whom were capable of the fraud'.

The final exposure of Wise did not come until the 1930s, when two booksellers, John Carter and Graham Pollard heard a rumour that the privately printed first edition of Elizabeth Barrett Browning's *Sonnets from the Portuguese* was not all it seemed to be. At the same time, they began to be suspicious that a large number of pamphlets of poems of roughly equivalent date had begun to turn up in auction sales and in the catalogues of certain booksellers and always in fine condition. They believed that somebody in the book trade had a large cache of this material and was releasing it slowly on to the market in order to keep prices up.

They also knew that one of these pamphlets, the text of a lecture by Ruskin, *The Queen's Gardens* of 1864, had been condemned as a forgery in 1903. Ruskin had given his lecture in Manchester in 1864 and the text had been printed in a Manchester newspaper the next day. It was published in a collection of Ruskin's essays, *Sesame and Lilies* in 1865. However, the text of the 1864 pamphlet did not correspond to those; it was in fact the amended text from the 1871 reissue of *Sesame and Lilies*. Clearly it could not be genuine. Carter and Pollard decided to investigate.

They decided to start with the Elizabeth Barrett Browning *Sonnets from the Portuguese*, because it was the most significant and valuable of the mysterious pamphlets – one copy sold in America for $1,250 at a sale in 1930. The pamphlet gave its place of publication as 'Reading' and according to the well-known Browning expert, Harry Buxton Forman, author of *Elizabeth Barrett Browning and her Scarcer Works*, it was the first known edition of the poems. Nobody had heard of this pamphlet until its discovery in the 1890s and a number had been sold at auction or in the trade since then. Amazingly, the known copies of the pamphlet were all in remarkably good condition and either unbound or in new bindings. Even stranger was the fact that there was a genuine 1850 edition of the pamphlet and Browning's original manuscripts dated 1850. But if the 1847 pamphlet was genuine, why would another manuscript need to be written for the 1850 edition? Something was not right.

Their efforts to trace the origins of *Sonnets from the Portuguese* all led back inexorably to Wise. However, they soon learned that many of the forgeries on the market in recent years had come from a Mr Herbert Gorfin. He had started as an office boy with Wise's essential oils company, but later set up as an antiquarian bookseller in London's Charing Cross Road. It was clear that Gorfin was not the forger, as he had been born in 1878 and was only 10 years old when the first known forgery was produced. However, he was quite frank with Carter and Pollard and explained that he had been Wise's agent, selling pamphlets on commission and that eventually he had bought all of Wise's stock. Of the pamphlets he bought from Wise, about half were forgeries. On the basis of Gorfin's evidence, Pollard and Carter approached Wise and described their investigations, giving him a list of suspect pamphlets. Wise did not reply and Carter and Pollard remarked 'We find it difficult to believe that Mr Wise cannot now guess the identity of the forger'.

They subjected a number of Forman and Wise pamphlets to detailed examination, the texts as well as the paper on which they were printed and the type used to print them. Up to 1861, all paper produced in England was made from rags, and pulp made from chemically-treated wood did not become available until 1874. The pamphlet of *Sonnets from the Portuguese,* which was dated 1847, turned out to have been printed on chemical wood pulp. Similarly, the type used to print it was identified as a type called No. 3 Long Primer, used by the London printing firm of Richard Clay in the early 1880s. Three of the letters in the type fount were known to have been cut after 1880. This pamphlet could only be a forgery.

John Carter and Graham Pollard published their findings in *An Enquiry into the Nature of Certain Nineteenth Century Pamphlets* (1934). The book is a remarkable piece of detective work and lays out in deadly detail the case against many of these mysterious pamphlets pointing the finger, indirectly, at Wise.

Carter and Pollard were very careful not to name Wise in their attack, as he was still alive and they were fearful of a libel suit. However, they were convinced that the group of forgeries had to be the work of one single forger and they pointed the finger at him through a heavy use of irony. When discussing the Ruskin forgeries they said, 'No doubt Mr Wise's preoccupation with his *Bibliography of Ruskin* in the years 1889–1893 provided an easy victim for the forger's wares'.

If they could not attack Wise directly for publishing forgeries, they were quite willing to condemn him for his failure to identify the pamphlets as forgeries and for his commercial activities. They drew attention to:

> *His original negligence in authenticating his finds; his purchase of them in bulk and subsequent gradual dispersal of them through commercial channels; his disingenuousness in emphasising the rarity of books which were not rare in the strict sense at all – all these things have inflicted damage in plenty on innumerable collectors all over the world, who have for years paid good money – and in some cases a good deal of it – for books which are, in fact, worthless except as curiosities ...*
>
> *In the whole history of book collecting there has been no such wholesale and successful perpetration of fraud as that which we owe to this anonymous forger. It has been converted into an equally unparalleled blow to the bibliography and literary criticism of the Victorian period by the shocking negligence of Mr Wise.*

It was all too obvious that most of the forgeries had come through Wise's hands – either directly or through the agency of Gorfin. A significant number of the forged pamphlets owned by the British Museum had either been acquired from Wise or from his employers in the essential oils business. A few of Wise's friends rallied round and the American bookseller Gabriel Wells printed a pamphlet defending him, sending copies to booksellers, collectors and librarians in England and the United States. The playwright George Bernard Shaw was amused by the whole affair and saw Wise's activities as a prank on collectors.

Wise did not defend himself seriously against this attack. However, his fellow conspirator Forman pretty nearly escaped. Carter and Pollard initially believed that there was only one forger, yet the year after their book had been published, evidence was found of the involvement of another person. An American manuscript collector had discovered a letter from Forman to Wise, which was heavily annotated by both conspirators and clearly showed the involvement of Forman in the crime. Since then, much more material has become available and it is now recognized that Forman was at least an equal partner to Wise. Various other people have, at times, been suspected of involvement too, including Forman's son, Maurice Buxton Forman and Sir Edmund Gosse, author of *Father and Son*. Gosse seems to have been exonerated and if Maurice Forman was a forger, he was a very minor one.

*   *   *

Sometimes attempts are made to resurrect the authenticity of documents long considered to have been forged. A well-known case concerns leather strips containing fragments of Deuteronomy, which Moses Shapira, an antiquities dealer from Jerusalem, claimed to have purchased from some Arabs in Jerusalem in 1878. Shapira gave three separate versions of the story of how he acquired the strips, but all included a claim that the Arabs had found them in a cave. Its location (if there ever was a cave) is not known. In 1883, he came to London and tried to sell the strips to the British Museum. Shapira had a record of selling forged artefacts and the best contemporary experts declared the strips to be forgeries. Shapira wandered round Europe for a few months and, eventually, shot himself in a hotel room in Rotterdam.

However, following the discovery of the Dead Sea Scrolls in a cave in Qumran, a number of scholars suggested that the whole question should be reopened. They felt that the texts of some of the Dead Sea Scrolls were similar to the Shapira fragments. With Shapira long dead and his fragments long missing, there seems little reason or opportunity for questioning the decisions of the critics.

Very occasionally, there are documents whose validity was once doubted but which were later proved to be genuine. One example is the Revels Accounts, discovered by Peter Cunningham, a scholar and antiquarian working in the Audit Office at Somerset House. Cunningham was searching through the vaults looking for material of Shakespearian interest, when he found a considerable amount of material, including the original accounts of the Master of the Revels for 1604–1605 and 1611–1612. In 1842 he published these accounts in a volume issued by the Shakespeare Society. The accounts were controversial among contemporary scholars, since they provided new evidence about the dating of several plays, notably *Othello* and *The Tempest*. However, they had the authority of the Shakespeare Society and its esteemed director, John Payne Collier, behind them.

Twenty-six years later, the world had changed. Collier had been unmasked as a forger and Cunningham had drink problems. He took the manuscripts to the British Museum, hoping to sell them. The museum was suspicious about their authenticity, but confirmed that if the documents had been removed from the Audit Office, then their proper home was at the Public Record Office (now The National Archives). The Deputy Keeper of Public Records took charge of them and wrote to Cunningham, saying that if he wanted them back, he would have to go to court.

So Cunningham lost his accounts, but he was soon to lose his reputation as well, since the reappearance of these documents was regarded with the deepest suspicion. The attack began in the *Daily News* in June 1868 – but at least the paper only claimed that Cunningham had been taken in. In the same year, the leading American critic Richard Grant White bluntly accused him of forgery. Cunningham did not sue for libel and by May 1869 he was dead. All the great manuscript scholars of the late nineteenth century – Madden and Bond of the British Museum, and Duffus Hardy of the Public Record Office – accepted that the accounts were fakes.

In the early years of the twentieth century, however, Charlotte Stopes and the psychiatrist and New York literary scholar, Dr Samuel Tannenbaum, took up the story. They had good reasons for suspicion. First, to a curator familiar with English manuscripts of the early seventeenth century, these accounts appear slightly strange – almost too good to be true. Second, the clerk who wrote the 1604–1605 account spelled the name 'Shaxberd' – a spelling unique among the 800 references to the playwright's name between 1550 and 1630. The spelling was odd – 'Duck' for Duke and 'Grinwidg' for Greenwich. In the 1611–1612 accounts the word 'called' is spelled with a single 'l', however, someone else has added the extra 'l', putting a curious sickle mark above the insertion. The 1604–1605 account recorded a play *The Winter Night's Tale* – an unknown variant of the title of *The Winter's Tale*. The 1611–1612 accounts record a performance of the *Silver Age* before the Queen and Prince Henry at Greenwich on the Sunday following Twelfth Night. Yet, the records of the Treasurer of the Chamber, which also record payments to players, make no mention of this performance and other records show the prince attended a different play in London that night, while the queen was also in London.

Curiously, despite these inconsistencies, evidence began to accumulate that the accounts might be genuine. In the 1880s, Halliwell-Phillips drew attention to a scrap of paper left by the great Shakespearean scholar Malone (who died in 1812) that seems to prove that Malone had seen the 1604–1605 accounts. The scrap even contains the spelling 'Shaxberd'. This was not conclusive, since the scrap is not in his handwriting, and some suggested that Collier forged it and added it to Malone's papers after his death.

In 1911, Ernest Law, a barrister and historian, and A.E. Stamp, Deputy Keeper of Public Records, set out to rehabilitate the accounts. They went through processes that they might have used had they been attempting to prove the documents were forgeries. First, Professor Dobbie of the Government Laboratories examined the 1604–5 accounts. He started by looking at the writing material and found that this was ink, not the water-soluble paint used by Collier for his forgeries. He also looked at the depth to which the ink had penetrated the paper and the rate of fading, concluding that the same ink had been used throughout the account.

Stamp looked in detail at the figures in the accounts too, and found that the totals corresponded to other accounting records at the Public Record Office. He then looked at the spelling and, in particular at the curious sickle sign over an added letter 'l' in the word 'called'. The accounts were signed by Sir George Buc, Master of the Revels and Stamp found other letters written by him containing a sickle sign to mark a double letter or an abbreviation.

Some of Stamp's arguments were quite weak, such as his claim that the strange patchy appearance of the writing in the 1604–1605 accounts was because the ink used had contained a lot of gum and was consequently very thick, cracking and flaking off over the years. Unfortunately, the accounts had been repaired (washed, flattened and treated with gelatine size) before they were examined and this rather weakened his case.

Equally, he had to rely on 'human error' to account for the differences between the Treasurer of the Chamber's Accounts and the Revels Accounts. Law is equally fallible. One piece of evidence concerned a reference in the Revels Accounts to a performance of *Love's Labours Lost* (by then an old play) in January 1605. Law talked about a letter from Sir Walter Cope to Robert Cecil mentioning a performance of the play in January 1605. Law pointed out that the letter had not been discovered until 1872 and so could not have been known to Malone or Cunningham or Collier. This is true, but unfortunately the letter does not refer to an official production of the play at court for which the Revels would have paid, but to a performance at a private house, for which they certainly would not have paid.

Despite the fragility of some of their arguments, it is now generally accepted that the accounts are genuine. Professor Schoenbaum, the great twentieth century biographer of Shakespeare said that the controversy over the Revels Accounts now appears to have been settled.

* * *

Some librarians and archivists have been reluctant to acknowledge problems with their holdings. According to W. Thomas Taylor, publisher, rare book dealer and author of the standard work on the Texas forgeries, a number of Texan institutions, including the State Library, were unwilling to prosecute when material had been stolen – material then used by forgers to produce further copies. He summed up their attitude: 'If there was a theft you kept it quiet at all costs'. The discovery of a forgery raises difficult questions about security and the status of the institution and there are further problems if the police become involved.

There can be even worse consequences. One of the few forgeries to have had an impact on current events was the Zinoviev Letter of 1924. This letter came at a sensitive time in British politics, when the minority Labour government had lost a vote of confidence for its decision not to prosecute a Communist writer, who had allegedly incited British soldiers to mutiny. Following the lost vote of confidence, the government called a general election and in this foetid atmosphere, four days before the election, the *Daily Mail* published the Zinoviev letter. This was claimed to have been sent to the Communist Party of Great Britain by Grigory Zinoviev head of the Executive Committee of the Communist International in Moscow and Arthur MacManus, British representative to the Communist International. It called for increased Communist agitation in Great Britain.

The election was a victory for the Conservatives, who replaced the minority Labour administration. At the time and for some years afterwards, the Labour Party blamed their defeat on the letter. Ramsay MacDonald, the Labour leader said that he had felt like a man sewn in a sack and thrown into the sea. More recent writers have claimed that, in reality, the letter seems to have had little impact on the outcome of the election, since Labour were not the big losers. They only lost 40 seats, leaving them with 151, while the Liberals lost heavily, falling from 158 seats to 118, and the Conservatives were the winners with a final total of 413.

The real impact of the letter was probably on Anglo-Soviet relations; the new Conservative government adopted a much harder line against the Soviet Union. It also may have had an impact on the Labour party which, according to some observers, preferred to blame their defeat on the letter, rather than addressing real political issues.

Zinoviev denied authorship within a short period of the letter appearing in the press, but the mystery of who wrote it has never been solved. Three *Sunday Times* journalists writing in 1967 pointed the finger at two Russian monarchists based in Berlin, who wished to undermine Anglo-Soviet relations, while the official Foreign Office historian, Gill Bennett, who wrote an account in 1999, also blamed White Russians.

Other forgeries have had equally major repercussions. The Donation of Constantine, the fourth century forgery granting the papacy dominion over the western Roman empire, was used by medieval popes to boost their territorial claims in Italy. The Protocols of the Elders of Zion contributed to the growth of anti-Semitism in Russia, the West and the Middle East. By a curious twist of fate, Heinrich Himmler, the subject of several forgeries, was responsible for notable forgeries himself, designed to blacken the reputation of Eric Rohm's Sturmabteilung or SA, the Nazi paramilitary Brown Shirts.

All the forgers discussed here were unmasked within a relatively short period and it is doubtful whether many people still believe the forged information. However, a few years ago, I published something on Shakespeare and was bombarded with mail from a man who was convinced that Collier's forged annotations on the famous Perkins Folio, were genuinely written by 'an old corrector'.

Some historians were inconvenienced and misled by the Hoffman documents, while dealers and librarians wasted money on the forged Texas broadsheets and the Forman-Wise pamphlets. A recently published edition of the letters of Noel Coward included two of Lee Israel's forgeries, without noting that they were forged. Drewe undoubtedly damaged those archives he attacked, yet the Himmler documents seem to have had little impact. Few people have heard the theory that Churchill murdered Himmler.

The biggest problems have been caused by Collier. Until quite recently, scholars suspected all the collections he had polluted. George Warner's article in the original *Dictionary of National Biography* said that 'None of his statements or quotations can be trusted without verifying and no volume or document that has passed through his hands ... can be too carefully scrutinised'. Collier was such a malign influence that even genuine discoveries have come under attack. In the 1950s, Sydney Race pursued a campaign against him in *Notes and Queries*, condemning even documents known before Collier brought out his editions of them. Now, however, thanks to the 15-year labour of Arthur Freeman and Janet Ing Freeman, the status of Collier's documents has been firmly established.

Forgery poisons the well of history. Journalist and historian Sir Max Hastings said of the Himmler forgeries, 'It is hard to imagine actions more damaging to the cause of preserving the nation's heritage, than wilfully forging documents designed to alter our historical record'.

And what of the future? Since about 2005 the British central government has created all its documents electronically, while many businesses, local authorities and private individuals also work digitally. This poses many problems for archivists. The National Archives has strict procedures for ensuring the integrity and authenticity of all digital records it acquires from government departments and other bodies. It measures the amount of data in a record before it leaves the department, transfers it securely using encrypted disks and then measures the data on arrival to ensure no loss of information. Once the data has arrived it is kept securely and monitored to ensure that no data has been lost.

All well and good. But the real problem is what is known as data integrity. How can an archive be sure that it is acquiring genuine digital records? The essential issue is that, unlike in the paper world, there is no 'original' in the digital world. If I send you an email and copy it to 20 other people where is the original, the copy kept on your machine or the one on mine? Problems can occur in all sorts of ways. In the simplest case, crucial data may have not been saved, or the archive may acquire an early draft of a document rather than the final version. In more sinister cases, an electronic record may have been corrupted or changed, either by a virus or by deliberate hacking. It is all too easy to change the address from which an email was sent or the name of the sender.

Collier and Hofmann 'found' their documents in libraries and bookshops. In the next few decades, perhaps their twenty-first century successors will find similar material on obscure hard disks that once belonged to a famous literary figure or will introduce their forgeries into the digital collections of a major library. They will discover that a degree in computer science will be of greater use than knowledge of ink and paper, but they will find too that the scope and opportunity for their activities is far greater than their predecessors could ever have imagined.

One final thought. It is very easy to fall victim to a forger – old books and manuscripts in our major collections do not normally come with health warnings. Distinguished scholars have fallen into this pit and it is not kind or necessary to name them. The historians most at risk are those who work on major figures – Shakespeare, Hitler, or even Robin Hood. As with all research, using archives and early printed records needs to be done with extreme care and any new discovery should be regarded with caution until proved genuine.

Chapter Three

Begging Letter Writers

Among the many varieties of mendacious beggars there is none so detestable as this hypocritical scoundrel

In 1756, John Fielding, the famous blind Bow Street magistrate published an article warning his fellow Londoners of the dangers of a class of persons he described as 'gamblers', though today we would call them cheats or fraudsters. Among the many types of rogues he identified were 'Sky Farmers': men who dressed like farmers and told sad (and entirely false) stories about losing their farms through fire or flood, leaving them destitute, with pregnant wives and sick children. According to Fielding, these men were in partnership with professional letter writers, who would send letters to benevolent ladies and gentlemen asking for their support for the ruined farmers. These begging letters were evidence of a type of criminal activity that probably began in the eighteenth century and continues today online.

To be a successful begging letter writer requires a shrewd perception of character. It is easy enough to write a simple request for money, but to achieve the highest profit it is necessary to demonstrate some connection with your intended victim. In the nineteenth century, some writers achieved this by pretending to be in the same line of business, or from the same social background as their target. Others would try to establish closer connections, claiming that their victim's mother had helped them in the past or that their son had served on a ship the victim had captained. It helps to have a shrewd knowledge of what is happening in the world and modern online begging letter writers quickly learn who has won the lottery or inherited a fortune or where the next hurricane is due to hit land.

Many people seem to have taken up this way of life accidentally; they would write a begging letter as a result of some personal distress, but if this was successful they would rapidly come to see that it was a possible way of increasing their incomes, even as a full-time occupation. Some of the writers we will look at seem to have had one strong idea, which they milked for many years. Alice Hammond, for example, had a complicated story about needing to bring her children back from Canada; Thomas Stone liked to pretend that he was a young friendless woman. Dickens believed that begging letter writing often ran in families, with children learning the trade from their parents. There were also suggestions that there were organized gangs of begging letter writers. In 1874 a letter in *The Times* talked of a gang of 50 begging letter writers, each of whom earned £5 a week. Apparently they had copies of directories, which were carefully annotated to show how likely people were to give money in response to a letter.

In the mid-nineteenth century, the use of begging letters was, to some extent, officially sanctioned. It was commonplace for struggling aspiring writers to send letters asking for support to someone more established in their field. William Makepeace Thackeray, the author of *Vanity Fair*, gave £500 a year to charity, much of which went to fellow writers, while Thomas Babbington Macaulay, the historian, was also known to be a soft touch. Sometimes there would be a public subscription for particularly deserving cases. When the writer Mary Russell Mitford's wastrel father died in 1842, Lord Radnor organized a public appeal through the newspapers for this 'solitary and almost destitute woman'. Enough money was raised to cover her father's debts of £900 and several hundred pounds she had lost due to a business failure.

Such appeals legitimized the use of begging letters, but there were clear and well-understood limits as to what was allowed. Genuine appeals by hard-up writers or down-at-heel clerks were acceptable. Once such people began to write letters on a large scale and also began to make entirely false claims, then they became of interest to the police. A good example is Henry Molineaux Wheeler, who founded a journal for clergymen's wives called *The Vineyard* and also wrote devotional works, but made his living by writing begging letters to the famous – from the Archbishop of Canterbury down to the Royal Literary Fund. The police estimated that he had made between £300 and £400 a year when he was arrested in 1870. He was sentenced to three months in prison.

In 1818 the Society for the Suppression of Mendicity was established by the Duke of Wellington and others to counteract the alarming prevalence of begging in London. Their aim was to encourage what would now be called responsible giving. The society employed a small team of constables, who would patrol the streets and detain beggars. If the beggars the constables encountered were genuine, they would be granted relief or advised of other sources of funding. If fraudulent, they would be taken before a magistrate to be dealt with as a vagrant.

Within two years the society set up a begging letter department to advise subscribers who had received begging letters whether or not they were genuine. The department rapidly got to know the names and handwriting of London's leading begging letter writers. In 1869, a similar organization, the Charity Organisation Society, was set up. Much of its work was trying to regulate and improve charities and to deal with fraudulent ones, but it too pursued individual begging letter writers.

One of the main benefits of subscribing to the Mendicity Society was that subscribers' names were published in the society's annual report. Begging letter writers soon learned from bitter experience that writing to a subscriber would result in a visit from one of the society's constables and a prosecution. They found it safer to harass non-subscribers who were less likely to call on the society for help. The society's work against fraudulent begging letter writers was one of its most successful activities. Even Queen Victoria used its services, doubling her subscription in 1857 in apparent gratitude for services rendered. It investigated and secured convictions of fraudulent begging letter writers for over 100 years.

The 1840s appear to have been the peak time for begging letter writers. The means was provided because of growing literacy – from 1833 central government began to fund schools for poorer children. The opportunity was provided by the introduction of a nationwide penny post in 1840. Suddenly, posting a letter became affordable for almost anyone and many people, including the criminally inclined, took full advantage. The motive was provided by increased poverty in the 1840s. The decade, known as the hungry forties began with an industrial depression, which saw many workers unemployed and continued with the Great Famine in Ireland which led to much immigration into England, putting pressure on resources.

In 1847, the Mendicity Society processed 8,000 begging letters and continued to handle over 4,000 a year into the 1850s. From the 1860s the numbers declined and about 1,400 a year were received in the 1890s. About a quarter of these were fraudulent, while another quarter were judged to be from people who were worthy of the society's support. The society put this decline in the number of begging letters down to its own activities. Anyone sending such a letter was risking prosecution.

Begging letter writing continued at about this level until the First World War. After the war, things changed rapidly – although the society was still handling about 1,300 letters a year in the 1930s, very few were fraudulent. Some members of the society put this change down to the introduction of unemployment benefit in 1911; others felt that the society's work had contributed to ending the abuse. In 1933, the Duke of Wellington, its chairman, said that the society had been formed to combat the horrible practice of fraudulent begging and from the figures the society had collected, it looked as though the practice had almost been conquered.

Begging letter writing was a minor irritation for most of its victims, but it touched a raw nerve with Charles Dickens. After his early success as a novelist, he seems to have given generously to almost everyone who contacted him and his support for some deserving cases encouraged others to give too. However, he rapidly learned that things were not always as they seemed and that an innocent desire to do good had led him to support all sorts of villains.

On one occasion, a persistent writer who had exhausted Dickens's generosity wrote to announce that he had enlisted with the East India Company and was off to Bengal. However, he had been advised by the sergeant of the regiment that he should take out a single Gloucester cheese weighing 12–15 pounds and he wanted Dickens to leave such a cheese out for him.

Another man whom Dickens helped was John Walker; he even sent his brother along to check that Walker really was in distress. However, Walker eventually went too far, claiming that his wife had died. Dickens again sent someone round to comfort him, only to learn that Walker was out, but that his wife was at home and in good health. Dickens handed Walker over to the Mendicity Society who arranged for him to be prosecuted. The experience was not a happy one for anybody. Although Walker had lied about the death of his wife, the magistrate discharged him, partly because there were some legal issues about the way he had been arrested, and partly because he really was in dire poverty. During the trial, Dickens began to feel sorry for Walker and was finally relieved that he had escaped punishment, but he became concerned about the impact the trial might have on his own reputation. He wrote 'I left the court with a comfortable sense of being universally regarded as a sort of monster'.

For Dickens, the final straw seems to have come with the case of the donkey. He had an old school friend, Daniel Tobin, who was down on his luck and whom he frequently assisted. In 1840 he made an extraordinary request:

> He had got into a little trouble by leaving parcels of mud done up in brown paper, at people's houses, on pretence of being a Railway-Porter, in which character he received carriage money. This sportive fancy he expiated in the House of Correction. Not long after his release, and on a Sunday morning, he called with a letter (having first dusted himself all over), in which he gave me to understand that, being resolved to earn an honest livelihood, he had been travelling about the country with a cart of

crockery. That he had been doing pretty well until the day before, when his horse had dropped down dead near Chatham, in Kent. That this had reduced him to the unpleasant necessity of getting into the shafts himself, and drawing the cart of crockery to London – a somewhat exhausting pull of thirty miles. That he did not venture to ask again for money; but that if I would have the goodness TO LEAVE HIM OUT A DONKEY, he would call for the animal before breakfast!

It is not clear whether Tobin was serious, or whether he was either deranged or winding up the great man. However, the incident seems to have cured Dickens of the desire to respond generously to begging letter writers. As a professional writer, Dickens could use his pen to take a form of revenge on those who had troubled him. In the 1840s he wrote a tirade in *Household Words* describing how he had been besieged for years by these crooks; how his attempt to bring a prosecution against one of them had failed and how few people ever took the trouble to report the matter to the police because they were embarrassed at having been imposed upon. He described the letters as one of the most shameless frauds and impositions of the age and complained of their authors' idleness, mendacity and the damage they did to the genuinely deserving. And he wanted them transported.

Dickens retained his hatred of this form of begging throughout the rest of his life. In his last completed novel, *Our Mutual Friend*, published in 1864–1865, he described how Mr Boffin, the 'Golden Dustman', is plagued by begging letter writers, including 'several daughters of general officers, long accustomed to every luxury of life (except spelling)'; men who threatened 'to make an end of themselves at a quarter to one p.m. next Tuesday if no Post-Office order is in the interim received from Nicodemus Boffin' and people who were too proud to accept a gift, but who would grudgingly accept a loan at 5 per cent per annum. There were the fantasists whose road to riches was only blocked by the lack of a particular thing – 'a clock, a violin, an astronomical telescope, an electrifying machine' and they would be condemned to abandon their hopes unless Mr Boffin sent them the money to buy one of these essential objects. In addition, letters came from country post offices written in a feminine hand: 'Dare one who cannot disclose herself to Nicodemus Boffin Esquire but whose name might startle him were it to be revealed, solicit the immediate advance of £200?'

Unlike Dickens, other victims took a more sardonic view of the matter. Baron de Rothschild had one of the largest collections of begging letters ever written to a financier. One writer offered to prolong the Baron's life to 150 years. De Rothschild replied that, although he had often been threatened with death if he did not hand over money, this was the first time he had been offered a longer life. He added that his religion taught that we are all under the hand of God and that he could not withdraw himself from God's decrees and so, regrettably, he had to decline the offer. However, he wished the writer well and congratulated him on the 150 years he had to live in the world.

Henry Mayhew, the journalist and social researcher, wrote about begging letter writers in 1863. He shared Charles Dickens's intense dislike for them: 'Among the many varieties of mendacious beggars there is none so detestable as this hypocritical scoundrel'. Yet Mayhew recognized that, like other scammers, these crooks required a set of skills. These ranged from good handwriting and grammar to an ability to produce forgeries of old documents, and a sound knowledge of potential targets – the nobility and landed gentry. The scammer also needed to keep careful records of his victims and the stories he had told them – telling the same hard luck story twice to the same person would be a disaster. Above all, he or she needed 'that shrewd perception of character peculiar to fortune tellers, horoscopists, cheap jacks and pedlars'.

Mayhew described the lies told by different categories of writers. One group were apparently broken down tradesmen who had lost money through the collapse of a bank in New York, the sinking of a ship, or a financial recession. Distressed scholars formed another category – their letters, adorned with erudite Latin quotations, asked for assistance to buy a new suit of clothes or travel expenses, so that they could take up a new job in the north of England. Then there were people who posed as decayed gentlemen – they had expected to inherit an estate, but dishonest lawyers and rapacious relatives had deprived them of their birthright. Their letters were lavish in descriptions of former prosperity: their father had laid down a good cellar in 1811 'the comet year', but they sometimes mentioned, with some regret, that they had lost heavily at Newmarket, Doncaster and Epsom. Their main skill was to claim some connection with their victims. In one case, Mayhew quoted a letter from a man who had met a relative of his victim when his regiment was in Malta.

This ability to convince their victims of some sort of connection between them lies at the heart of all the really successful scammers. As we will see, the Spanish Prisoner was also a master of this approach, as were many of the writers quoted by Mayhew. He cites an example of one crook who wrote to a scholarly vicar fond of architecture, claiming that he was the son of an architect who had lost his life in the wreck of the *Charon*, a US packet boat. He then wrote to a man who was keen on the abolition of the slave trade, explaining that he was a tradesman from America who had lost his fortune helping female slaves to escape. Next he found a literary gentleman who wrote plays and novels and told him that he was a bookseller whose shop had burned down and, in between all of these other letters, he wrote to the wife of a sea captain, informing her that he was a widow whose son was formerly the purser on her husband's ship the *Thetis* and had been drowned off the Cape. Although he managed to get £5 from the captain's wife, his hopes for more were dashed when her husband turned up and exposed the lie.

Sometimes the police would arrest begging letter writers and when they searched their rooms they would find complex notebooks containing details of possible victims – often members of the aristocracy or politicians. Others tried adverts in the newspapers. In 1852, Thomas Henry Stone placed an advertisement in *The Times* under the name Miss T.C.M., saying that he was a young and unfortunate lady who was friendless and had been driven to the utmost distress. An architect called Richard Foster took the bait and wrote to Miss M., who replied that her name was Frances Merton and that she was the daughter of a merchant. She had been in good circumstances, but after her father died she had got into difficulties. Foster was hooked and sent her money.

More begging letters came. It turned out that Frances had a child of her own – she had been seduced by a base villain and needed money to have a nurse care for her child while she worked. Frances offered Foster other temptations. If she could have a little more money, to enable her to get a better lodging, she would be happy to have Foster call on her so she could tell him her life story. Intrigued and excited, Foster sent more cash. He was clearly totally gullible, since Frances insisted that all his letters should go to the Post Office in Cromer Street off the Gray's Inn Road.

Stone's next target was Samuel Whitbread, the brewer, who was not so easily fooled and reported the matter to the authorities. Stone was caught collecting one of Foster's letters from the Post Office, he was arrested and his rooms searched. The authorities found a large number of letters on similar themes signed by Fanny Hamilton, Fanny Lyons, Mary Danvers and Mary Whitmore. At his trial it turned out that he had previous convictions, having previously defrauded the Duke of Wellington of £450. He was sentenced to be transported for seven years.

Perhaps the most villainous begging letter writers were those who preyed on the recently bereaved. Mayhew quotes an example of a letter received by a newly widowed woman. The author 'Kate Stanley' claimed that the widow's late husband was the father of her young son and that he had been sending her a regular payment for quite a long period.

Writing to those who had just lost relatives was a common approach for many criminals. In the 1930s, Henry Theodore Green, a former schoolmaster from Cardiff, was convicted of obtaining money from a widow, Doris Kirk of Blackpool. Green had got the name and address of Mrs Kirk and his many other victims from death notices in newspapers and had written to them claiming that he was an old acquaintance of their late spouses who was down on his luck and needed help. Half his story was true – at the time of his trial Green was down on his luck and living in a hostel for the destitute.

Like Green, many begging letter writers seemed to have lived in a marginal world of cheap lodging houses and hostels. In 1908 a man called John E. Thompson, or John Vaughan, or sometimes John Bourne Jones, was convicted of writing begging letters; at the time, he was living in a lodging house in Drury Lane. The most respectable of the places offering accommodation for poor people were the Rowton Houses, set up in the 1890s by the philanthropist Lord Rowton. They provided homes for some of the letter writers. John Ernest Hilton, convicted in 1919, was living in a Rowton House in the King's Cross Road. James McGhee, convicted in 1926, resided in another on Arlington Street, Camden Town. George Orwell met one such man in a lodging house, who:

> wrote pathetic appeals for aid to pay for his wife's funeral, and, when a letter had taken effect, blew himself out with huge solitary gorges of bread and margarine. He was a nasty, hyena-like creature. I talked to him and found that, like most swindlers, he believed a great part of his own lies.

Some begging letter writers were not particularly successful in their chosen trade. William Yates was one of these. Born about 1797, he started life as a mathematical instrument maker, but soon found an easier way to make a living – or so he thought. In 1828, he was transported for seven years for writing begging letters and probably got back to England in 1835. Between then and 1842, he was convicted six times of begging-letter related offences. Yates was a particularly mean-minded criminal. In 1838, he was prosecuted for sending out begging letters appealing for funds to help a Mrs Mary Pilbeam, whose house in St Pancras Road had burned down and two of her children killed. Mrs Pilbeam was genuine, as was the fire, but Yates had no connection with her and gave her no money. He was convicted again of sending begging letters in September 1841 and was released from prison in December of that year.

While in prison Yates came up with a new scheme. He thought he would go round various charities, the Magdalen Hospital, the Foundling Hospital and the Seaman's Society pretending to be the secretary of a lord. He would bring along a letter from the lord saying that he wished to subscribe to the charity, and a cheque for the subscription. However, he would explain that the lord being an absent-minded man had written out the cheque for too high a sum. Would the charity mind giving him the change in cash? The charities obliged and only found out they had been defrauded when the cheques from the lord bounced.

Inspector Pearce of the Yard realized that the letters were written by an expert and wondered if the fraudster might not be a begging letter writer, so he took them along to Mr Knevett of the Mendicity Society, who recognized Yates's handwriting at once. Yates was arrested, tried at the Old Bailey and sentenced to transportation for life, leaving England for the last time on the *Surrey* in March 1842.

Writing begging letters is not a physically demanding job and many of the best writers seem to have been able to pursue their chosen profession for very many years. Alice Hammond of Bexleyheath was a long-term begging letter writer. She first came to the attention of the authorities in 1912, when she persuaded Mrs Fry to give her £5. Mrs Fry's husband, the Reverend Fry of Bexleyheath, complained to the Charity Organisation Society. During the First World War, Hammond tried a little thieving, but in the 1920s she settled down to a life of begging letter writing. She was quite indiscriminate in her approach and sometimes she wrote to members of the aristocracy, including letters to the Duke and Duchess of Rutland, the Duchess of Portland and the Countess of Dalkieth. On other occasions she went after wealthy businessmen. Duncan Elliott Alves, owner of Bryn Bras

Castle in North Wales was one of her targets. His secretary told the police that Alves had received many of these letters and had been many times deceived.

Alice Hammond was quite unscrupulous. In 1925 she heard that Mrs Jones Bennett of Bickley had lost her husband soon after her wedding. She wrote, claiming that Mrs Bennett's husband had helped her by funding her children's passage to Canada, and asked her to send her another 15 shillings. However, she sometimes backed the wrong horse entirely. In 1927 she heard that Mr J.W. Brook of Meltham Hall had died intestate, leaving a fortune. She wrote off claiming that Mr Brook had helped her in the past. This was simply fantasy – Mr Brook had spent the last 60 years of his life being cared for in the Ticehurst Mental Hospital.

Hammond's basic technique was exemplified in the Brook case – she would claim some connection with her victim in order to gain extra sympathy and get them on side. Just as we will see in the next chapter how the Spanish Prisoner claimed to be a relative of his victim, so Hammond would claim that her victim's mother, father or husband had helped her in the past. If she was writing to a duchess, she would not fail to mention that another equally grand lady had recently helped her by sending her £10.

Although the police described Mrs Hammond as a cunning, plausible fraud, she sometimes behaved foolishly. In 1926 she wrote a begging letter using her maiden name of Bunyan and in 1932 she used her daughter's maiden name. The police were not fooled by the false names because she put her own home address in Bexleyheath on the letters. Yet they found it difficult to persuade people to testify against her and so for most of her life she was simply cautioned and allowed to carry on.

However, in the 1930s she tangled with Edward James, the art patron of West Dean, Chichester. She probably learned about him from a newspaper article. In 1934 James was involved in a sensational divorce, in which he accused his wife, a ballerina, of adultery and she counter-sued for homosexuality and cruelty. Never one to miss an opportunity, Mrs Hammond sent him two letters asking for £40 to bring her daughters back from the United States. True to form she claimed that James's mother had helped her during her husband's long illness before he died and afterwards had helped her with her 11 children. Despite his reputation for eccentricity, James was no fool and noticed a couple of suspicious features about the letter. First, he noted that her earlier letter had not mentioned the friendship with his mother and second, he observed that Hammond described his mother as an American. A simple misreading, which was to cost her dear – in fact James's mother was Scottish and it was his father who was an American.

James's secretary passed the letter on to the Charity Organisation Society who contacted the police and, eventually Hammond was sentenced to three months' hard labour. But Hammond could not give up her old ways and in 1936, she read that a Mrs Dunlop had left £34,000 in her will. She fired off her usual letter asking the widower for money to bring her children home from Canada. The police became involved again and in 1938 she was sentenced to three months with hard labour. The policeman who investigated the case, Detective-Sergeant Heath, said she was one of the most accomplished begging letter writers in the country.

Much remains unknown about Mrs Hammond – it is not certain how many children she had – sometimes there were five and sometimes eleven. Some of them may have moved to Canada or the United States. But the big mystery is why she wrote so many begging letters. It was certainly lucrative; the Charity Organisation Society believed that she made £100 from one victim and £40 from another. However, she was not short of money, her husband was a bricklayer and found regular work around north Kent. Their house was well furnished and they had few financial worries. She did not appear to drink heavily. She said that she spent her ill-gotten gains on furnishing the house and educating her children.

When questioned by the police, her husband claimed to have been ignorant of her activities. As well he might have been since on at least two occasions she wrote asking for money because he had just died. Sadly, her real motivation will remain a mystery. She last appeared in Metropolitan Police records when she was cautioned yet again for writing begging letters in 1946, some 34 years after her career began. At the time of her arrest she was in the middle of writing a letter to a Mr Drabble asking for money.

Wartime provided additional opportunities. During the First World War there were many examples of letters from 'wounded soldiers' and even holders of the Victoria Cross. The writers scoured the casualty lists and sent letters addressed to recently killed soldiers asking for the repayment of a loan or for a gift of a few pounds to an old comrade down on his luck. The bereaved relatives, confused and distressed would often oblige.

Although the trade was in decline by the 1920s, the methods of the writers remained the same – the wealthy and those whose names appeared in reference books were still targeted – the King and the Prince of Wales received letters in 1924. In 1926 George Edward Cave was convicted of sending out letters – he was found to have registers of Uppingham and Harrow Schools in his room.

In the late 1930s, Harry Clapham, the vicar of St Thomas's, Lambeth, was running a major scam. He had an office in the basement of his vicarage with staff, typewriters, addressing machines and 91 bank accounts to support his business of sending out a million begging letters a year asking for funds for his church. The resulting income supported a lifestyle of foreign travel and the purchase of property across London. Arrested in 1942, he was sentenced to three years' imprisonment.

Those lucky enough to win large fortunes also became targets. In 1927, Mr William Kilpatrick had a half share in the winning ticket in the Royal Calcutta Turf Club Sweepstake on the Derby; his winnings probably amounted to about £60,000. As a result, his name was published in the papers and he received over 4,000 begging letters; he fled London to return to his native South Africa, where he resumed his trade of dental mechanic.

The practice still continues, now with lottery winners as the victims. In 2008, Jane Surtees from Whitby won £7.5 million on the lottery. Initially she planned to keep her fortune secret, but one of her daughters told a school friend and the secret was out. She was an immediate target. 'One guy wrote to me asking me to pay off £600,000 of debts from his daughter's wedding. I didn't spend nearly that on my own this year', she said.

Naturally the internet provides a good hunting ground for the modern begging letter writer. It seems that every natural disaster is followed by many fake appeals for donations to help the victims. These scams are so well-known to the authorities that major hurricanes in the USA are followed by a tsunami of warnings from the Federal Emergency Management Agency, the Department of Homeland Security and others about the folly of donating other than to reputable charities.

Even before Hurricane Sandy made landfall in New Jersey in 2012, more than 1,000 new websites were registered with the words 'Sandy', 'relief' or related keyword search terms in their addresses. Some were created by construction companies, lawyers or repair companies for potential business opportunities. But most, say experts, were opened by scammers; many of whom wanted to direct well-meaning but unsuspecting people to fake charity websites and collect their money. A different world, but Fielding's Sky Farmers of 1756 would easily spot their fellows a quarter of a millennium later.

Chapter Four

The Spanish Prisoner

We sent this money as we thought there was a girl and in that troubles [sic], out of sympathy for the child and they have proved a lot of roughs and we have loss [sic] all what we have worked for

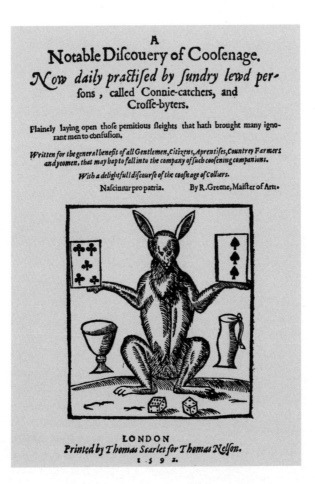

A

Notable Discouery of Coosenage.

Now daily practised by sundry lewd persons, called Connie-catchers, and Crosse-byters.

Plainely laying open those pernitious sleights that hath brought many ignorant men to confusion,

Written for the general benefit of all Gentlemen, Citizens, Aprentises, Countrey Farmers and yeomen, that may hap to fall into the company of such coosening companions,

With a delightfull discourse of the coosnage of Colliers.

Nascimur pro patria.   By R. Greene, Maister of Arts.

LONDON
Printed by Thomas Scarlet for Thomas Nelson.
1 . 5 9 2.

Have you received an email from Nigeria offering you a share in a fortune? Perhaps it was from the son of a disgraced politician or a banking official. They needed your help to get some money out of the country. The money had been obtained illegally and you needed to be very discreet in dealing with them. If you were intrigued enough to reply, then you would soon have been asked for the details of your bank account so you could be paid your share of the loot. Alternatively, you may have been asked for some money to help fund the transfer.

If you replied and seemed co-operative, then you might have been invited to visit them in Nigeria or another African country, where, if you were lucky, you would have been kidnapped and ransomed; alternatively you might have been murdered. The email you received was the latest example of a scam that has been going on for over 200 years and which is variously known as the 'Spanish Prisoner', the 'Advanced Fee', or the '419 scams'.

The first example I have been able to find of the scam was reported by Eugène François Vidocq in 1797. Vidocq was an extraordinary figure. He started as a criminal, yet went on to found the French equivalent of Scotland Yard, the Sûreté Nationale, and later ran a private detective agency. As a young man Vidocq was imprisoned in Bicêtre prison, near Fontainebleau. While there he noticed that some prisoners were making money by practising a trick called the 'Letters from Jerusalem'.

The letters were sent to wealthy people and were allegedly from the valet of a marquis who had escaped from the dangers of the French Revolution carrying a cask filled with gold and diamonds. The marquis and his valet had found themselves pursued by revolutionaries and had been forced to throw the cask into a deep ditch. They eventually escaped abroad and the valet had come back to recover the treasure. Unfortunately, the valet had been arrested and was in prison; he was so short of money that he would have to sell a trunk which contained a plan showing the location of the treasure-cask. However, if the recipient could him send some money the valet would send him the plan and they could share the treasure. By a strange coincidence the recipients of these letters always lived close to the place where the money was hidden.

The scam was hugely successful; about 20 per cent of the letters were answered and many people came to the prison and were supplied with treasure maps. One cloth seller from Paris was so convinced by the whole business that he began digging under an arch of the Pont Neuf, believing the treasure was concealed there. By the 1870s this idea had made its way to Spain and on 21 March 1877, *The Times* of London reported that some swindlers there had tried to obtain money from a number of people in various parts of Scotland, by promising to reveal the whereabouts of large quantities of hidden treasure. This report is the earliest reference in a newspaper to one of the biggest and best organized frauds ever, and one that exceeded the current Nigerian email scams in both scale and ingenuity.

This fraud, known as the 'Spanish Prisoner', continued from 1877 until the Spanish Civil War. It was so well-known that it turns up in James Joyce's *Ulysses*, when Leopold Bloom is imagining how to obtain a fortune. He starts with the possible – finding a very valuable postage stamp. He then turns to the improbable and among the possibilities he considers is the likelihood that an eagle in flight might drop a valuable antique ring, or that one might be found in the gizzard of a comestible fowl. Even more fantastic is the possibility of a Spanish Prisoner's donation of a distant treasure lodged with a solvent bank 100 years previously at 5 per cent compound interest.

The success of the scam was due not only to the professionalism of the fraudsters, but also to their considerable psychological skills; their letters had the remarkable ability to appeal to both their victims' greed and to their better feelings – a winning combination, which ensured a ready stream of profits for the scammers in Barcelona for 60 years.

The method was simple: a letter would be sent to the intended victim from a man claiming to be a prisoner in the Castle of Valencia. He had been a captain and treasurer of a Spanish army regiment, but after stealing a large sum of money, he had fled to England where he buried the money – usually near the home of the intended victim. The captain had left behind a wife and daughter in Spain, but the wife had died and the man had returned to Spain to care for his daughter. Unfortunately, he had been arrested and sentenced to a period of imprisonment. His daughter was a student in a college in Spain and he was very concerned about her. However, there was a solution at hand. If the victim would send some money to cover travel costs, his daughter and her governess would set off for England bringing with them a map showing where the treasure was buried. For security reasons, the victim should not write direct to the prisoner, but to a third party, usually either the prisoner's servant, or more frequently, the chaplain of the prison.

Illustration by 'Phiz' from Charles Dickens's *Little Dorrit*: Once he knew that he and his banking empire were doomed, Mr Merdle borrowed a knife from his stepson and daughter-in-law and took it to the bath house where he killed himself.

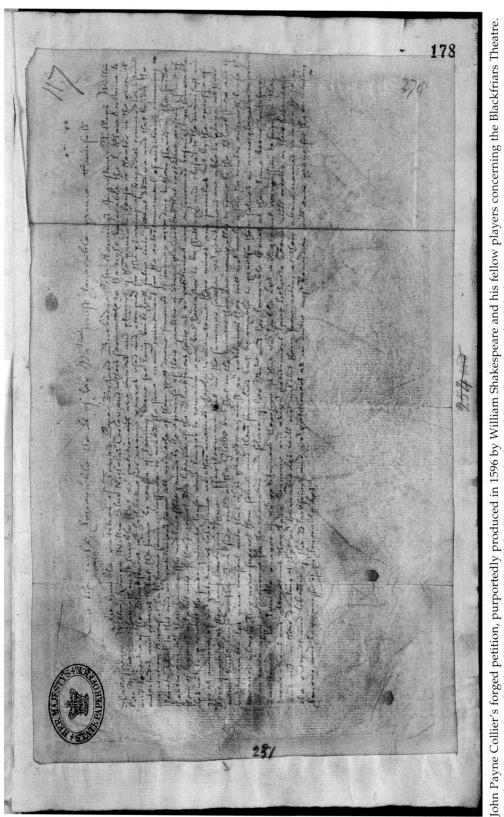

John Payne Collier's forged petition, purportedly produced in 1596 by William Shakespeare and his fellow players concerning the Blackfriars Theatre. The forgery was revealed by the mention of the Globe Theatre (which could not have been built before 1598) in line 13. *(TNA: SP12/260/178)*

We, the undersigned, at the desire of the Master of the Rolls, have carefully examined the document hereunto annexed, purporting to be a petition to the Lords of Her Majesty's Privy Council, from Thomas Pope, Richard Burbadge, John Hemings, Augustine Phillips, William Shakespeare, William Kempe, William Slye, Nicholas Tooley, and others, in answer to a petition from the Inhabitants of the Liberty of the Blackfriars; and we are of opinion, that the document in question, is spurious.

30th January, 1860.

Fran. Palgrave KH
Deputy Keeper of H. M. Public Records
F. Madden K. H. Keeper of the Mss. Brit. Mus.
J. S. Brewer, M.A. Reader at the Rolls.
T. Duffus Hardy, Assist. Keeper of Records
N. E. S. A. Hamilton, M.SS. Brit: Mus.

I direct this paper to be appended to the undated document now last in the Bundle, marked 222. Eliz: 1596.
2 February, 1860.

John Romilly
Master of the Rolls.

Confirmation that the 1596 petition (on the facing page) was forged, signed by Sir Francis Palgrave, Keeper of Public Records; Sir Frederic Madden of the British Museum; J. S. Brewer of the Rolls Chapel; Thomas Duffus Hardy of the Public Record Office; N. E. S. A. Hamilton of the British Museum; and endorsed by Sir John Romilly, Master of the Rolls, 30 January 1860. (*TNA: SP12/260/177*)

Rd. Dec 16

9 Rowan Rd
BExley Heath - Kent

Dear Mrs Jones Bennett

I hope you will excuse me writing to you in your great
sorrow. I was shocked at reading of your husbands death
Please believe me how sorry I am for you. Mr Jones Bennett
as been a kind friend to my husband and helped several
of the children by paying part passage to Canada. We have
had great distress for several years & my husband as been ill
for several months

We wrote last week to Mr Jones Bennett to see if he could help
us with 15/- we are in great need of as he all way had done
I am so sorry to ask at such a time as this, your husband
may have explained to you we need part of the money
for hospital treatment and nursing home and to get him
things to go with until such time the children can send
money home. Please believe me how sorry I am for you
at so near Christmas and so soon after your wedding as he
was so very kind to all who knew him. Dear Mrs Jones Bennett
forgive me asking about the money now at such a time
only our distress is terrible, as he as Cancer of throat
& internal trouble & need great care to keep from choking as your
husband as all way help my husband in several occasions I trust

---

Begging letter from Alice Hammond to Mrs Jones Bennett of Bickley, 1925. Mrs Hammond had
heard that Mrs Jones Bennett had lost her husband soon after their wedding and wrote to her asking
for a loan of 15 shillings to support her husband who, she claimed, had throat cancer.
(TNA: MEPO 3/1440)

you can do this for us. & as soon as children send home I will return back to you. I have 11 children in all The 4 eldest in Canada Vancouver. I have sent and ask them to send home what they can. Pray God will give you strength to bear your heavy burden of trouble, I am so sorry for you and my husband as he was one of the best friends he ever had. God Bless you in your great trouble but thank God dear Mrs Jones Bennett thank God he as not had suffering like my dear Husband we all have a heavy Cross to bear in different ways May God comfort us both in our time of great Trouble Please forgive me writing now only I wanted to know about the money by Friday to get things for Hospital if you can find time to answer God bless you for your kindness I am yours truly

Mrs Hammond.

The second page of the letter from Alice Hammond to Mrs Jones Bennett: Mrs Hammond claimed to have 11 children, but the number varied from letter to letter. Her husband also seems to have made a full recovery from his imaginary illness. *(TNA: MEPO 3/1440)*

The interior of a room inside Watts's charity in Rochester: Visitors were impressed by the charity's cleanliness but sometimes upset by the draughts.
(Courtesy of Hope Thomas)

Elaborate steps were taken to add an impression of credibility to the story. The letters were often accompanied by copies of printed 'official' documents, designed to add a degree of authenticity. In 1904, William E. Jack, a Lancashire businessman, was pursued by a man calling himself Augustin Rosales. Their correspondence lasted three months and Jack was sent extracts from newspapers announcing the arrest and then the death of the prisoner, a death certificate and legal documents relating to his will. Clearly, the gang had huge resources to invest in reeling in their victims.

These features – a prisoner, a hidden treasure illegally acquired, an unfortunate daughter and a third party to whom the intended victim should write – are typical of virtually all the Spanish Prisoner letters. Details varied: in 1877 a gunsmith in Birmingham received a letter from a man who had buried a large fortune somewhere in the West Midlands. This time he was not a treasurer of a Spanish regiment, but an arms dealer, who had been trying to acquire weapons for the Carlist rebellion in Spain when he had to flee, because the British authorities were becoming suspicious. In other cases, there are letters from an absconding banker, who had hidden a large amount of money in a secret compartment in a suitcase. He had been arrested and the suitcase confiscated by the prison authorities, but it could be recovered if a suitable bribe were paid to his gaoler. At other times, there were mentions of a large legacy.

Sometimes the gang tried other variations on this theme. In 1910, a man in Anderson, Indiana, received what was claimed to be a newspaper cutting from a London paper. It contained a story about a Russian banker who had fled from St Petersburg with five million roubles. He had gone to Spain, where he shot and killed a fellow Russian in a fight. He then moved to Britain, where he was arrested by a Spanish policeman accompanied by two Scotland Yard officers, while on his way to book a passage to New York. At this point in the story it became apparent that this really was a Spanish Prisoner scam – the Russian was a widower with a daughter, whom he had left in Spain. When the police searched his luggage, they found little of interest, but the Russian ambassador was convinced that he had several million roubles hidden somewhere. Curiously, most of the surviving copies of these letters are in the United States – perhaps the gang felt that a Russian prisoner would be of greater appeal there.

The early letters were very skilful – the victims were being offered large amounts of money, but this had been obtained illegally so they were pretty sure to keep quiet about it. They were also being asked to help a poor motherless girl, whose father was imprisoned in some terrible castle in Spain. Sometimes, it seems that the victims were motivated by a genuine sense of compassion for the poor daughter of the prisoner. In 1908, R.W. Carter of Montgomery wrote to the Foreign Office saying that he had sent money in response to a Spanish Prisoner letter, 'we sent this money as we thought there was a girl and in that troubles [sic], out of sympathy for the child and they have proved a lot of roughs and we have loss [sic] all what we have worked for'.

Although many people responded and many lost money, the letters lacked something – a reason why the victim had been chosen. After all, even quite naïve people might have their suspicions raised if a letter from an unknown Spanish prisoner suddenly arrived out of the blue. So the fraudsters, who were great experts in human nature, began to add a little twist. In 1908, Edwin Maund, butler to Sir Richard Harrington, received a Spanish Prisoner letter claiming that the writer's deceased wife had been Mary Maund, a relative of the butler. In the same year, William Bennett of Dublin and Mrs J. Mann of Bulpham Hall, Romford, Essex, also received letters from long-lost Spanish relatives offering access to large fortunes, in return for a small initial payment.

The claim that the prisoner was related to the victim was very powerful. In 1911, A.E. Dilke of Wells, Somerset, told Scotland Yard that he had received a letter from Spain and had responded because 'I had relatives in Spain several years ago and through my parents being both dead, I could not find out where they were. I thought perhaps it was something to do with them'. Dilke was lucky, he had sent £95 to an address in Madrid, but Scotland Yard sent a telegram to the British Embassy in Madrid who contacted the Spanish Post Office, who managed to recover the money before it was delivered to the fraudsters.

The skill with which the victims were lured into the gang's web is illustrated by a letter sent to Edgar Paul of The Manor, Wroxhall, Dorchester in 1897, allegedly on behalf of a Leopoldo Garcia of Valencia. Garcia wanted the reasonable sum of £20 for a share in his fortune. He urged Paul to be careful; 'for more security it is necessary you have the letter registered at the Post Office, taking care to seal well the letter with sealing wax'. Once the money had arrived, Garcia's wife and daughter will set off and also send Paul a photograph of the daughter. They will travel to Maiden Newton Station and on arrival, carry a black handkerchief so that Paul will recognize them. These details – the need to register the letter and to seal it with sealing wax, as well as the promised photograph and the mention of the black handkerchief are calculated to create an air of mystery and excitement and to turn Mr Paul into a co-conspirator with the gang. Unfortunately, Paul fell into the trap.

Another man who was totally seduced by the fraudsters was Thomas Sinclair of Falmouth, who in 1893 wrote a long and pompous letter to the Foreign Office about the case of Thomas Swanson d'Aigular, a prisoner who had died in Melilla – the Spanish outpost in northern Morocco. He had left £100,000 and a daughter, Laura. Sinclair was quite convinced that the facts in the letter accorded with what he knew of his family – he believed that Thomas Swanson's father was his uncle. He demanded that the Foreign Office take action to protect the daughter and stated that 'the case seems beyond the possibilities of the clearest imposition'.

Sinclair was just another victim of the Spanish Prisoner. The Foreign Office wrote back to him, pointing out that they were aware of another letter concerning a Thomas Jones d'Aguilar, who had died a year before in Melilla prison. When they had contacted the Spanish Director General of Prisons he had assured them that no such prisoner had existed. The Foreign Office's response was both formal and totally crushing to Sinclair: 'the case to which you draw attention does not appear to Lord Rosebery to be one that calls for the intervention of Her Majesty's Government'.

Not every victim was so easily fooled and not all of them took the matter very seriously. Some people even tried to fight back. Several wasted the time of the gang by engaging them in a long and ultimately futile correspondence. Others had more pressing priorities: the Reverend Addison of Coltishall was not concerned about the possible swindle; instead he was anxious that the police should return the stamps on the envelope in which his letter had arrived because one of his family was a philatelist. Edward Behrens, a well-known businessman, received a Spanish Prisoner letter from Mexico in 1948. He wrote to his friend Ronald Howe, who was Assistant Commissioner for CID at Scotland Yard:

My dear Ronnie
I enclose a letter which we discussed over the telephone the other day.
Don't be a hog and keep all the 449,000 dollars for yourself.
  Yours ever
  Edward

There was a spate of letters in 1920, and an official who saw one asking for £150 remarked that the Spanish Prisoner was one of the notable survivors of the war and that his demands were one of the few things which had not gone up in price.

One interesting question was why did the gang not try to disguise the fact that they were Spanish? Surely, I thought, most people must have heard of the Spanish Prisoner swindle, so why not make up a new name, try a new fraud or disguise the fact that they were from Spain? In fact, they stuck to pretty much the same story, with a few minor variations, between 1877 and 1948 – a period of 71 years. I assumed that all but the most naïve and foolish people must have heard that a letter from a Spanish prisoner was a trick to part them from their hard-earned money.

It was only when I began to investigate the Nigerian email fraudsters that I began to understand. From the point of view of the gang, hooking and reeling in a victim was an expensive process. Sending out the initial letters was cheap, since they could be mass-produced. However, if they got a response from a possible victim, then they had to engage in a correspondence with them to persuade them to hand over their money. This required a gang member who wrote good English and was able to answer the specific queries raised by the intended victims. Most of the letters I have seen are both well-written and persuasive. Evidently this part of the process was costly and time consuming.

From the gang's point of view, the trick was to identify the likely prospects at an early stage. If the gang did not disguise themselves but were quite open about sending out letters as Spanish Prisoners then, yes, only the most innocent and foolish people would respond, but it was precisely those people who were the most likely to send money to Spain. The whole exercise was quite remarkable – the victims selected themselves and then, because they were doing something immoral if not illegal, they entered into a co-conspiracy with the fraudsters. What could be better than that? As we shall see, these techniques have been adopted in recent years by the Nigerian scammers.

Also the fraudsters were not afraid to use the latest technology of their era. In the early years of the twentieth century, they began to encourage their victims to respond by telegram. This had two advantages – it was quick and, because the victims had invested money in the price of a telegram, they had already begun to buy into the scam. The Spanish authorities began to intercept these telegrams in 1906 and passed them to Scotland Yard. However, they rarely contained the addresses of the victims and there was little the Metropolitan Police could do to prevent these people from sending money to Spain. The intercepted telegrams provide evidence of the enthusiasm with which people bought into the fraud. Charles Clark, a bicycle dealer from Lewisham received a letter and immediately telegrammed back a message with the rather mysterious text 'All your wishes'. When the fraudsters failed to reply within a few days, he wrote asking for more information. Clark was lucky – he had given his home address in his telegram and the police were able to track him down before he sent any cash.

Less fortunate were Charles Green and Richard Henry Mather, both of whom sent telegrams agreeing to the fraudsters' proposals and we can only suppose that they handed over their money, but received no treasure and no daughter in return.

Sometimes the criminals seriously miscalculated. In 1908, using a method they could have learned from a Sherlock Holmes story, they encouraged potential victims to place advertisements in the personal columns of the *Daily News*, showing that they were interested in their proposals. Fortunately, the editor was wise to their tricks and when William Crouch of Peckham tried to place an advertisement, he advised him to consult Scotland Yard.

Little is known about the people behind the scam; criminal gangs are very poor at record-keeping. Even the city from which they operated was a mystery. In 1889, the Home Office noted that the swindle was spreading to Segunto, Valencia, Madrid and Alicante. However, by 1906, the Foreign Office remarked that nearly all the letters they had seen had been addressed from Barcelona and they concluded that the Catalan capital was the headquarters of the gang.

What was obvious to everyone who looked into the case was that the fraudsters had a large and efficient team. As baffled British officials noted, the very varied handwriting on the letters showed the size of the organization. In 1906 a Home Office official had spoken admiringly of the splendid organization of the swindlers and in 1934, C.D.C. Robinson of the Home Office wrote 'the business is obviously organised on a fairly extensive scale and clearly involves an elaborate filing system and a good deal of expense'.

What is certain is that the gang sent out a large volume of letters and made a huge income from the scam. Unfortunately, they did not leave accounts and we can only use other traces to estimate the scale of their operations. We do not know how many letters were sent or received, but there are some clues. In 1897 an average of six letters a week from the Spanish Prisoner were sent to the Dead Letter Office in London as being undeliverable. In 1904 the British Consul in Barcelona reported that 'the Spanish Swindle seems to be unusually brisk, not a day passing but what letters a propos of it reach this Consulate General from Great Britain'. In 1915 and 1920 the British postal authorities intercepted two mail bags, each containing 300 letters from the swindler.

Great Britain was not the only country subject to the gang's attentions. One of the most interesting features was that they had a global reach. In the nineteenth century, letters were sent to Australia, Germany, Switzerland and the US. In the decade before the First World War there is also evidence of letters going to Canada, Denmark, South Africa, France, and the Netherlands.

We also have some evidence about the amount of money that the gang was handling. In 1897 the Commercial Banking Company in Sydney reported that they had stopped payments of £885 because they had been obtained by fraud on their customers. In the same year, William Wyndham, the British Consul in Barcelona, reported that he had heard from his German colleague that in one month, the Credit Lyonnais in Barcelona had cashed bankers' drafts for nearly £3,000, which the bank suspected were connected with the swindle. He also noted that there were large numbers of English bank notes in the hands of money-changers in Barcelona; these had probably been sent by innocent victims in Britain. On the basis of these pieces of evidence, he concluded that the gang was making £500,000 a year; this is equivalent to about £29 million today.

In 1910, Major Arthur Griffiths, a British Inspector of Prisons, published a book on Spanish prisons. In it he describes how a cache of stock-in-trade of the gang was seized in Granada. It included a great mass of information, including standard letters in various European languages intended to be sent out to potential victims. He also gave a further insight into the way Spanish fraudsters operated when he described a knife fight in Ceuta Prison, after one prisoner had stolen a picture of the sister of a fellow convict. Apparently the thief intended to use the picture in a buried treasure swindle – he planned to pretend that the picture was of a marchioness and was intending to use it to demonstrate his acquaintance with the aristocracy and thus pave the way for a scam.

What is certain is that the Spanish Prisoner could not have worked without huge co-operation from staff employed in the Spanish Post Office. The fraudsters sent letters to England, suggesting that the victims get in touch with someone other than the prisoner – usually the chaplain of the prison or the prisoner's servant. However, these were fictitious people who were not known at the addresses given. Often the addresses themselves were false. Clearly post-office officials were intercepting the letters addressed to these fake individuals and passing them on to the criminal gang. Even senior officials were implicated. In 1897 the Spanish postmaster general revealed that one of his predecessors had been offered £150 a month by the gang for keeping quiet about their activities.

The post office workers also acted as the eyes and ears of the gang. In 1899, the Chief Constable of Gloucestershire, Admiral Henry Christian, wrote to the Home Office about two Spanish Prisoner letters which had been sent to farmers in Gloucestershire. The Home Office forwarded the letters to A.F. Ivens, the British Vice-Consul in Valencia. Ivens passed them on to the city's chief of police, who decided to set a trap for the gang. The letters suggested that the intended victims should write to a Candido Gonzalez. The police visited the address given in the letters, but Senor Gonzalez was not known there. So the chief of police persuaded the director of Valencia Post Office to send a letter to Gonzalez, inviting him to come to the post office, where an insufficiently stamped letter would be handed to him. A policeman was stationed in Valencia Post Office ready to arrest Gonzalez when he showed up. Gonzalez never made an appearance and Mr Ivens ruefully commented that the swindlers had been tipped off by accomplices amongst the post office staff.

In 1904, a Mr Goddard of Bath foolishly sent £20 in a registered letter to an Emilio Bores of Barcelona. When he realized his mistake he contacted the Spanish postal authorities, who claimed to have no record of a registered letter to Bores. The British and Spanish authorities then decided to set a trap – Goddard sent another letter to Bores to be collected at the local post office, but the suspect (who had presumably been tipped off) never showed up.

Not all Spanish postal officials were in the pay of the gang and there was considerable co-operation with the British authorities. In 1908 they compiled a list of known fraudsters and intercepted letters addressed to them, returning the money to their intended victims. Henry Fink of Balham had sent £175, which he was lucky enough to get back courtesy of the Spanish Post Office. In 1920 they intercepted several bags of mail, which they believed were fraudulent, and handed them over to the British authorities.

One of the most interesting questions is how did the gang identify their potential victims? The letters were addressed to individuals and often made play of the fact that the recipient had connections in Spain. There were two schools of thought – both of which have some validity. The view of the Foreign Office and, indeed, of some of the victims was that the gang had agents in various countries who were tasked with fingering likely people to approach. In 1894, the British Embassy in Madrid suggested that the gang had accomplices in Britain, because many victims were often obscure persons living in remote villages. In 1897, H. Drummond Wolff, British Ambassador to Madrid said that:

> *there must be a reason at all events in certain cases for the choice of the persons intended to be dupes, perhaps some ancient or acquaintance connection with Spain, as it seems impossible that the writers should select names at hap-hazard over the United Kingdom on mere chance of a successful response.*

In 1911, William Tomlinson, a mining engineer from British Colombia and recipient of a Spanish Prisoner letter, wrote to Scotland Yard: 'some letters show a close personal knowledge of the history or personal affairs of the parties to whom the letters are sent'.

The Home Office were not convinced that the gang had agents in Britain. They believed that they got the names of potential victims from directories; usually quite out-of-date ones. Had the gang been using agents or up-to-date directories, then fewer letters would have ended up in the Dead Letter Office. Sometimes the gang made the sort of mistake that would have been unlikely had they been using local agents. In 1906 they wrote to a William Topley, who had been dead for 22 years. In the same year they contacted the husband of Mary Bates, a newsagent of Compton Street, London, who had been dead for seven years.

Even odder mistakes were made; in 1908 the gang wrote to Harry Robertson of Mincing Lane in the City of London. Robertson had received four separate Spanish Letters in his lifetime. This one made him laugh because it claimed the prisoner was married to Mary Harry, a distant relative of Robertson's. As Robertson said, 'the assumed relationship through my Christian name is new and rather amusing'.

We know the names of many intended victims through their correspondence with the Foreign Office or Metropolitan Police. It is normally possible to identify them in Post Office directories and it seems clear that the gang had copies of these. It seems that in the early years of the twentieth century, the gang also got their hands on a clerical directory. In 1901 there was a spate of letters to Anglican vicarages in Abingdon, Aberystwyth, Ackworth, Addlestone, Ambleside, Alford. Clearly, the addresses came from *Crockford's Clerical Directory* or something similar. The British Consul in Barcelona wrote to the ambassador that they had received five letters from clergymen in England: 'all the letters date from places beginning with 'A' and Your Excellency will observe the Bs are to be attacked next'. Indeed the Embassy soon received a letter from a clergyman in the Somerset parish of Berrow, concerning a letter he had received from Spain promising him a huge treasure. As a result Scotland Yard put a notice in newspapers entitled 'A warning to clergymen', giving details of the scam.

The gang also had access to Catholic directories and made use of them as well. In 1907 the Archbishop of Westminster wrote to the British Consulate in Madrid about a mysterious letter, which had been received by the Mother Superior of the Sisters of Mercy in London's East End. The letter indicated that the community had become entitled to a legacy under the will of Mr William Griggs, who had died in Spain. The Mother Superior was asked to send cash to defray legal expenses. All the letters to clergymen and nuns seem to have been about a mysterious legacy – presumably the gang calculated that the recipients would be less enthusiastic about an offer of stolen treasure.

However, there is evidence that there were also agents operating in England. In 1895, a Mr Dubois, a French Confectioner of Baker Street, received a letter from Spain. It was the usual story – a prisoner, a daughter, a treasure buried in England. Dubois approached the police and agreed to work with them to try to trap the perpetrators. The CID wrote back in Mr Dubois' name and strung the gang along, promising to hand over the money requested, if they could provide more proof about where the treasure mentioned in the letter was buried.

The gang gave such clear directions that they could only have been written by someone with detailed local knowledge. To find the treasure you needed to take a train from Charing Cross to Orpington. Then, leave Orpington Station and turn right on Bromley Road, walk on until you reached a sign post and then take the Chislehurst Road. After a few paces, you had to take a little path on the left hand side and in 100 paces, you would see two oak trees on the right-hand side. Close by would be the trunk of a tree. The treasure was apparently buried within 25 yards of the tree trunk. Its precise location, however, would only be revealed in a letter that the prisoner's daughter would bring to England.

Inspector Charles Arrow of the CID was intrigued by the letter and so he went to Orpington and followed the directions. He eventually found the two oak trees and the trunk of another. He reported that he did not find any treasure, but the police were convinced that the description could only have been written by someone who had visited the place. Incidentally, if this information has inspired you to buy a spade and take a train from Charing Cross to Orpington, you need to be aware that the place where the oak trees grew is now occupied by housing. However, the Spanish Prisoner's treasure may remain buried there, perhaps under a patio!

One question worth exploring is whether there was one gang or several. The British authorities always talked about a gang, implying one group, but the issue seems not to have been properly discussed. My belief is that there was one main gang, because running a Spanish prisoner scam was hugely expensive. There has been some recent published discussion of the Nigerian scam, which indicates that the costs of running a similar business are very high.

The first stage, sending out the letters was relatively cheap, yet things got progressively more expensive after a potential victim had taken the bait. Then, they would have to be reeled in, often using a series of letters, so people with good linguistic skills were required and in many cases specially printed documents – wills or death notices – were produced. In addition, lots of officials would have to be bribed and there were overseas agents to maintain. Finally, the money received would have to be exchanged for Spanish currency and either banked or hidden. It seems unlikely that more than one gang would have been able to afford the huge infrastructure needed to run the scam on the scale we have seen.

The British government departments dealing with the fraud, the Foreign Office, Home Office and the Post Office, approached the problem with a mixture of uncertainty, dithering and a lack of sympathy for the victims. Part of the problem was that they misjudged the scale of the crime – in 1898, a year after the Foreign Office had estimated that the scam was worth £500,000 a year, the Home Office justified inaction on the basis that the scam was not very successful. Moreover, they were very ready to condemn the Spanish officials, from the Barcelona Post Office to the civil governor and the magistracy. They were also simplistic in their view of the difficulties the Spanish police faced in capturing the gang.

William Wyndham, the British Consul in Barcelona, wrote 'I am very much surprised as are also my colleagues, that as yet the swindlers have not been found at the places and addresses which I have many times given'. The truth is that every time the Spanish police raided an address named in a Spanish Prisoner letter, they found no evidence of the gang – the letters from England were being intercepted by the gang's accomplices in the Barcelona Post Office.

Many officials were deeply unsympathetic to the victims, believing them to be foolish and naïve. In 1895 Drummond Wolfe, the British Ambassador to Spain concluded tersely, 'this particular expedient for obtaining money from credulous individuals is now so well known that little sympathy can be felt for those foolish enough to be taken in'. In 1921, Esme Howard wrote from the British Embassy in Madrid that: 'it is a source of wonder to me that people can be so foolish as to send considerable sums of money in notes to unknown persons in a foreign country on so slight a provocation'. He reported that the French had decided to take no action to protect people who showed such lamentable gullibility; while the American Embassy was equally unwilling to do anything constructive.

Perhaps the most prescient of the British officials to comment on the swindle was F.C. Ford, Ambassador to Spain, who wrote in 1887, 'There is little likelihood of seeing it abolished so long as there are dupers in the world and persons desirous of enriching themselves by any means on the strength of the most absurd and preposterous of stories'. How right he was.

However, British officials all felt under pressure to do something to save the victims from their own folly. The first and most obvious thing to do was to warn potential victims. From at least 1895 there were regular letters in the newspapers from either Scotland Yard or the British Ambassador in Madrid, containing warnings about the prisoner scam with a detailed description of the gang's methods. Sometimes copies of the letters were sent to Scottish and Irish newspapers and to governors of British colonies. These were supplemented by notices displayed in post offices. Mostly the letters contained standard descriptions of the fantastic story told by the prisoner, but occasionally they had new information. In 1915, Scotland Yard said that 'he has now become a Belgian who, on the death of his master at the siege of Liege has fled to Spain with £20,000 of Bank of England notes'.

The most obvious way of dealing with the swindle would have been to simply stop the letters from being delivered, or to intervene to prevent replies being sent. Here, however, the forces of law and order and the General Post Office came into collision. The Post Office had a strong tradition that the post should always get through and they were not about to interfere with their service just because of a few Spanish swindlers. In fact, their powers to delay or open letters were very restricted.

In the nineteenth century, officials could open letters for the purposes of detecting crime, preventing crime of a treasonable nature and preventing the degradation of morals by the dissemination of obscene matter. In the case of obscene publications, they could not prevent their delivery. Instead they opened envelopes being sent to the suppliers of such material and confiscated the money they contained. They were unhappy about doing this. More generally they were reluctant to interfere with fraudulent mails, raising every obstacle they could. Checking the post from Spain would cost an extra 30 shillings a week, even if their staff could identify the scam letters, and that would be hard because they were written in so many different hands. Even when they were asked about putting up notices in post offices to warn people of the risks of letters from Spain, they initially refused to help. They did not have enough room on their walls and the Spanish Prisoner was not a subject they were concerned with.

On the occasions when they did try to help the victims they did it in a bureaucratic and ham-fisted way. In early November 1914, Frank Henry Woods, a builder and undertaker of Albury, near Guildford, sent £135 to a Señor Alonso of Valencia. On 8 November he realized that he had been tricked and approached the police. They spoke to the postmaster in Guildford who referred the matter to Post Office Headquarters, where a supervisor and two sorters spent a couple of hours looking for the letter, which they found in the bag bound for Barcelona. The Post Office in London decided that they had no legal authority to detain the letter and so they sent it on to Barcelona and asked the authorities there to investigate it and return it, if fraud was suspected.

In February 1915 the Spanish authorities agreed that Mr Woods' suspicions were well-founded and agreed to return the letter to London. The Post Office told Mr Woods that he would only get his money back after he had paid them the seven shillings and two pence they had spent on finding his letter and also provided proof that he had, indeed, posted it. Eventually in March 1915, four months after he had sent it, Mr Woods received his money back.

Things changed in the First World War, because all foreign mail was subject to censorship and the censors found many Spanish Prisoner letters. The Post Office wanted to be able to return such letters to Spain, but the Home Office was unwilling to allow them to do this. Instead, the Post Office instructed postmen delivering the letters to warn the recipients that they were fraudulent. In August 1915 the Post Office raised a further problem. The censors had found some envelopes containing Spanish Prisoner letters which were being sent via London to the British colonies. They were concerned that it would be impossible to warn people receiving these letters that they were scams.

Frustrated by the Home Office's refusal to allow them to return the letters to Spain, they held a gun to their head by writing to them, 'we propose to forward these letters to their destinations in ordinary course. Perhaps you would let me know whether you see any objection to this'. Eighteen days later they received Home Office approval to detain all letters from Spain relating to the scam. They retained the theoretical power to detain Spanish Prisoner letters up to the 1930s, although this was fairly ineffectual, since, with the ending of censorship, they were not allowed to open envelopes even if they had grounds for suspicion.

While those people who sent money off to the gang were unfortunate, all that they lost was cash. A few foolish individuals set off to Spain to rescue the prisoner's daughter and recover the treasure for themselves. This seems to have happened a number of times because the Spanish authorities put up posters in railway stations and hotels warning travellers in several languages of the Spanish Prisoner scam.

Major Griffiths told the story of a Hungarian restaurateur called Elked, who was persuaded to go to Madrid with 10,000 francs in the hope of getting a fortune of 300,000 francs, part of which was in a trunk in the cloakroom of a French railway station and part in the strong room of a Berlin bank. Elked met the representative of the gang, who persuaded him to send telegrams to the bank and railway station. In due course, replies arrived confirming the existence of the trunk and the bank deposit. He was satisfied by these telegrams and agreed to meet in a café to hand over the money. Fortunately, Elked had met a fellow Hungarian called Isray on the train journey to Madrid. Isray realized the whole thing was a fraud and so, armed with a revolver, he followed Elked to the café and was able to rescue him from three gang members, who were trying to get him into a carriage.

In a similar case in 1934, a Dane went to Barcelona in the hope of getting a chest full of jewels and valuable documents, as well as a cheque for £2,400. He handed over £380 to the gang, but the chest did not exist and the cheque he was given was forged.

Even worse treatment was meted out to a senior member of the Catholic Church who, according to Major Griffiths, visited Ceuta to assist in the rescue of a former general who knew the whereabouts of a huge treasure. The priest went to an address given to him by the gang, where he was beaten up and only escaped with his life because the gang were concerned about the possible impact of murdering a senior cleric. In 1910, Arthur Train published a short story in *Cosmopolitan*, which described how a group of strangers travelling on a boat from the US to Spain came to realize that each of them was on their way to rescue an unfortunate Spaniard who was in prison, also intending to acquire a share in his fortune and marry his impossibly beautiful daughter.

One of the constant complaints that the British police and Foreign Office made about the Spanish Prisoner was the inefficiency of the Spanish courts and police. They believed that the Spanish officials lacked the vigour to deal with the problem. In 1903 the British Embassy in Madrid passed a collection of Spanish Prisoner letters to the police, hoping that these would provide them with clues. Six months later, Frederick Adams of the Embassy wrote to the Foreign Office in London saying that no progress had been made in the case. He claimed that the letters that had been passed on to the police contained much evidence – the handwriting was often the same, the same phrases were used and many of them gave addresses in Madrid. He wrote, 'I think the correspondence certainly furnished enough clues for the Spanish Police Authorities to work upon with good prospect of success if they had chosen to take up the matter energetically or if they had shown any ingenuity in following up the case'.

Adams was perhaps being unfair to the Spanish authorities. As we have seen the gang was large and well-organized, with agents in the Post Office and it is doubtful that the letters supplied to the Madrid police were of much help. The Spanish police made a number of arrests. In 1894, a man called Rico who was allegedly the leader of the gang was arrested, but his first lieutenant, Ricardo Tascon Garcia de la Pena, escaped. A year later, a man identified as Eusebio Martinez shot himself while evading arrest; he was found to be carrying a Spanish Prisoner letter. In 1903 the *Evening Standard* carried a report that the ringleader had been arrested.

Arresting people was only the first problem facing the Spanish police. The second was persuading their British victims to come to Spain to testify. There are a number of cases in the Foreign Office files where the Spanish police had a man in jail, but his British victims refused to testify. Even if the police could make an arrest and get sufficient evidence, the Spanish courts did not regard this crime as particularly serious and typically would impose small fines on persons who were convicted.

Occasionally the civil authorities tried to intervene. In 1897 the Civil Governor of Madrid told the British Ambassador that he had written to the courts complaining about this situation but had been told not to interfere. In the same year, the Spanish Ministry of Grace and Justice wrote to the presidents of the courts of Valencia and Barcelona, urging them to take action in these cases: 'It is unnecessary to mention to Your Excellency how prejudicial to the good name of our country in foreign lands is this system of fraud in which Spain appears to have the sole and exclusive privilege'.

By the early years of the twentieth century, things were as bad as they ever had been. The new governor of Madrid was not interested in the crime; trials were postponed, the accused were allowed out on bail and the Crown Solicitor only asked for fines as low as £10 or even less. In 1907 there was a general amnesty, which resulted in the release from prison of a band of men who had been arrested on the advice of the German embassy. This gang was important because the letters they sent to Germany were written in the same handwriting as letters sent to England – clearly they were at the heart of this scam and were now on the loose again.

The truth is that the Spanish authorities shared the same ambivalent attitude to the scam as the British, believing that the crime was only possible because of the attitude of the victims. In 1909 the Spanish Ministry of Foreign Affairs wrote to the British Embassy:

The police here have no pity for those who are swindled by such a well-known method and one in which the party taken in is not a mere innocent victim of an inevitable fraud. They do not therefore enjoy the role of guardian angels over the defrauded persons and consider it is the business of the latter not to allow themselves to be taken in by such absurd methods and by the mirage of fabulous wealth easily acquired.

After the First World War, the gang gradually came under threat – largely because of the actions of Spain's two military dictators. Up to the 1920s, Spain had been desperately poor and badly governed. In 1923 Captain General Miguel Primo de Rivera led a military coup overthrowing Spain's elected government. Originally promising to govern for 90 days, Primo de Rivera stayed for seven years. Like Mussolini in Italy, he tried hard to modernize Spain with public works and a stronger administration. In 1926 he introduced changes to the Spanish penal code, including making it a specific offence for persons to offer a share in fictitious treasure or valuables in exchange for money or securities.

This did not entirely deal with the problem and there were still Spanish Prisoner letters in the 1930s. Barcelona, home to the scam, was a stronghold of anarchists and socialist trades unions and staunchly supported the Republican side in the Spanish Civil War. There is no evidence of a direct link between the anarchists and the Spanish Prisoner gang, but it is possible the gang operated with their consent. It seems likely that the disruption to the Spanish postal service caused by the Civil War made the work of the gang more difficult, while the fact that Spain was constantly in the newspapers in the 1930s made the whole scam less credible. In any event, after Barcelona fell to General Franco's forces in January 1939, there were no more Spanish Prisoner letters – at least not from Spain.

However, some of the gang members had set up a subsidiary business in Mexico. In 1934 and again in 1940, the US Consul in Mexico issued press notices warning that the swindle was being carried out there. At least one man had travelled south from the US and paid over $3,000 to the gang. In 1948, Scotland Yard received mailbags full of letters from well-educated people enclosing mysterious letters they had received from Mexico, which all told a familiar story about a man and a treasure and a daughter in an orphanage. It is almost certain that the Prisoner had got the names of his intended victims from *Who's Who*. We know this because one of the letters was addressed to Joseph Todd Macleod. Mr Macleod told the Yard that he rarely used his second name and that the gang must have got it from a reference work, such as *Who's Who*.

By using *Who's Who*, the Prisoner had hit on the wrong group of victims – the people on his list were intelligent and well-educated and few of them can have been taken in. This was probably the last major outbreak of the Spanish Prisoner letter scam, what subsequently happened to the gang is not known.

One tempting theory is that the legacy of the Prisoner can be found in the spate of emails from Nigeria and other places in Africa now clogging email inboxes. Ironically, in 1914 Sir Arthur Hardinge, the British Ambassador to Spain, wrote to the Colonial Governor of Nigeria warning of the dangers of the Spanish Prisoner scheme and suggesting that the public in Nigeria should be encouraged to be on their guard. However, it is hard to establish a real connection between the Spanish Prisoner and the letters and emails known as 'Advanced Fee Scams' or 'Nigerian 419 Scams', after the section of the Nigerian criminal code relating to them.

The way these scams work is that an email is sent from a person claiming to be a government official or a senior person in a company. The writer claims that there is a large sum of money in a bank account, which was put there as a result of overpayments on contracts, and he asks the help of the recipient in transferring the money to a legitimate account in Europe, in return for a percentage of the funds. All the unsuspecting recipient has to do is to send his/her bank details and later some real money to facilitate the transfer.

If the recipient replies and gives banking and personal details, he or she will be sent fake bank statements and similar documents, all intended to prove that the money exists and is heading their way. The scammers might use the information given them to empty the victim's bank account or they might convince them to send cash up front.

The emails often mention the names of real people. Some, for example, have claimed to have access to the secret bank accounts stashed abroad by the late President Mobutu of Zaire. Others claim to be from the son of the late Sani Abacha, a former military ruler of Nigeria. Others claim to have links to the victims of tragedies – in 2000 a number claimed links to the victims of the Kenya Airways A310 crash. Like the Spanish Prisoner letters, these emails have considerable emotional appeal. They are written in a crude way, with poor grammar and awkward phrasing. This seems to be designed to convince the recipient that the writer is naïve and innocent. Then, like the Spanish letters, they seek to draw their victims in by a mixture of charity and greed. Often the victim is encouraged to believe that they are helping someone in Nigeria, but that they will also be well rewarded. The noose is tightened by a strict insistence on secrecy – the transaction is portrayed as illegal and so security must be maintained.

More recent emails have focused more on the charitable aspects of the scam. A Mrs Amanda Harper recently indicated that she was dying of a serious blood disease and had chosen me to help give her fortune to charity. All I needed to do was to send her my personal details. Curiously, on the same day a Suhail Mitwally wrote to tell me that he was rich and sick and had chosen me to give his fortune to charity. My benevolence must be famed worldwide.

The success of these scammers is hard to estimate. In 2011 it was guessed that the cost of online fraud to individuals in Britain was £1.4 billion. An earlier survey showed that in 2006, 70,000 people were victims of these Advanced Fee scams at a cost of £340 million. Many people lost large amounts – the average amount paid over was £5,000. Surprisingly, the typical victim of this crime was a male, between the ages of 45 and 65, from a higher or middle social class and living in London. About a third of these unfortunates would lose further money in another scam within a year, mainly because their details had been added to 'suckers' lists passed around criminal gangs.

The victims normally learned that they had been conned when warned by friends and colleagues, or when they realized that their money had not arrived. Others only found out by checking their bank accounts. About a tenth of the victims went on to report the crime to police or other authorities, but alarmingly, 3 per cent or over 2,000 people refused to accept that they had been cheated.

There are other similarities with the Spanish Prisoner scam. One is that the gang sometimes encourages the victims to travel to Nigeria or elsewhere in Africa to meet them. Such visits end badly with the victims being kidnapped, tortured or murdered. In 2004, a 29 year old Greek, George Makronalli, got involved with a gang which claimed to have stolen £10 million from the government by submitting false claims for contracts. He flew to Johannesburg to help them smuggle the money out of the country. A few days later, his brother received a ransom demand for £80,000. This was not paid and a day later the police found George's body in Durban. His arms and legs had been broken and he had been set alight, probably while he was still alive.

There are other Advanced Fee frauds that relate closely to the Spanish Prisoner's method. They include lottery scams, where criminal gangs will send out emails telling people that they have won a large cash prize, government payout or other major award. Most sensible people ignore such messages, but a few reply. These people will receive a second message telling them that to claim their winnings they must send a fee of between £5 and £30, variously described as a 'processing', or 'administrative' fee. Naturally, no prize money (or only a trivial amount) is forthcoming. Another variant is the credit card scam, in which a person will receive an email telling them that they are eligible for a pre-approved credit card or loan. A fee will be charged in advance. There is no card or loan, simply a scammer waiting to take their money.

Some potential targets have begun to fight back. There are websites devoted to the sport of scambaiting, where recipients of Advance Fee emails reply using assumed names. Their intention is to waste as much of the scammer's time as possible, so that the scammer will not have the chance to attack other people. The more experienced scambaiters have a range of tricks they can use to delude the scammers, including persuading them to visit the local Moneygram office to collect non-existent transfers of funds and even persuading them to go to the airport to meet their (imaginary) victims arriving on real flights. A good example (which includes some photographs of scammers) is at *www.419eater.com*. However, scammers have links to violent criminals and while baiting them looks like jolly fun, there are risks involved. Some of the sites give some good tips on how to bait scammers safely.

These frauds rely on a combination of greed and generosity. Greed because what is being proposed is clearly illegal; generosity because the victims of both frauds can justify their involvement because they are helping someone less fortunate than themselves, whether it is a poor girl in a Spanish orphanage or a simple, barely literate person from Nigeria. Even the victims of the credit card and lottery frauds are motivated by greed. If they thought about it carefully, both groups of victims would admit that they had never entered the mysterious lottery which was going to bring them a huge fortune, or that, in the real world, banks do not issue cards without careful credit checks.

The scammers are masters of psychology, drawing their victims into a web of deceit, a skill common to all practitioners of this black art.

Chapter Five

Sturdy Beggars

Imposture like every other trade, requires for thorough success a long apprenticeship and a keen observance of the foibles and weaknesses of human nature

A Soap-eater, copied from a rare print of the time of Queen Elizabeth p 18

A Tom of Bedlam copied from an Old Drawing of the time of Edw: 6 in the possession of Fran: Douce Esq See p 20

Copied from a Drawing of the time of Henry VIII in the possession of Francis Douce, Esq See p.27.

This chapter is concerned with 'sturdy beggars', people who, though capable of working, choose a life of idleness and begging and develop elaborate techniques for persuading passers-by to give them money. They are of interest to us because, as the fabled Clause Patch, the 'King of the Beggars' said on his deathbed, 'Our community, like people of other professions, live upon the necessities, the passions, or the weaknesses of their fellow creatures'. The psychological tricks sturdy beggars use to get money are very similar to the tricks used by the other cheats described in this book.

Beggars learn that the simplest way to get someone to give them money is to ask them for it, but most people will not respond to such a simplistic request and so, at the minimum, they need to look miserable and bedraggled. But many people will not react to this either and some further technique is needed. As we will see, being accompanied by a child, preferably a ragged and unhappy one helps (but this has been illegal in the UK since 1889). Alternatively, you can get more sympathy by appearing to be sick and we will learn about the various dodges beggars used to feign disease. At the extreme, a beggar could make himself or herself so repellent that people would pay them money to go away – pretending to be insane was a favourite trick up to the nineteenth century. There are alternatives to appearing to be ill. We will learn how beggars with good current affairs awareness took full advantage of tragedies, ships sinking and towns burning down.

But there are more subtle methods; one technique was to demonstrate some link to your intended victim. Beggars often pretended to have been respectable people who had fallen on hard times when calling on the middle classes or tradesmen who had lost their businesses when calling on shopkeepers, and soldiers or sailors when calling on colonels and captains. Then there was snobbery and approval. The ideal way to beg was to get some sort of endorsement from an aristocrat; a reference from a duke would open all sorts of doors. Finally, a few – a vanishingly small number today – of beggars try to use humour.

How do we react to beggars? This seems to have changed over time. Writers from the sixteenth to the eighteenth centuries liked to frighten their readers by describing an organized underground of vagrants and beggars full of clever tricksters bent on cheating honest citizens. At almost all periods, beggars have been seen as work-shy, idle and not above a little petty pilfering. In the nineteenth century, there was a curious outbreak of nostalgia for beggars – more bureaucracy, better policing and improvements in welfare had driven the more colourful characters off the streets. But, as we will see, most beggars are not members of organized gangs or petty thieves. The majority are poor people down on their luck and we cannot know the truth of their situation.

Exact numbers of beggars, vagrants or rough sleepers are hard to calculate and most figures need to be treated with caution. It is difficult to identify the numbers of beggars and rough sleepers at any one time and the basis on which calculations were made has changed frequently. Moreover, most people tramping from place to place in the nineteenth century were genuine work-seekers; it was common for navvies to walk to the next major construction site or merchant sailors to walk from port to port. In 1806, a London magistrate, Patrick Colquhoun estimated that there were a total of 70,000 tramps, gypsies and beggars, as well as 10,000 wandering performers and another 10,000 lottery ticket touts, out of a total population for England and Wales of 10 million.

The number of beggars clearly increased after the end of the Napoleonic Wars in 1815, with many displaced soldiers and sailors on the roads. Coldbath Fields House of Correction received 265 vagrants in 1810, but 1,287 in 1820. However, the number of vagrants declined as the economy improved in the 1820s. The numbers swelled in the 1840s because of agricultural depression and the impact of the Great Famine in Ireland; the workhouse in Stafford saw admissions rise from 3,178 in 1843 to 11,108 in 1847. The number of vagrants declined once more, later in the nineteenth century, due to increasing prosperity, but numbers rose in the early 1890s because of the economic depression, only to fall during the Boer War, rising again with the return of soldiers from the war in 1902. There were 5,000 people in casual wards in workhouses on 1 January 1884; 8,300 on the same date in 1894; 5,600 in 1900; and between 8,000 and 9,000 in 1905.

The First World War led to a dramatic decrease in people on the roads, because there were more jobs and fewer men of working age. Consequently, only 1,091 people spent 1 January 1918 in the casual ward of a British workhouse. The depression following the Wall Street Crash of 1929 led to an increase in the number of people moving about to seek work and in May of that year 16,911 people spent a night in a casual ward in England and Wales. Thereafter, the numbers declined – Labour Exchanges meant that there was less need to tramp around looking for work and assistance was given with railway fares for people looking for jobs, while the dole provided a basic level of financial support.

After the Second World War, there was, at first, a decline in the numbers of single homeless people, with the number of rough sleepers declining to fewer than a thousand in 1965. But more recent figures are difficult to interpret and highly politicised. In 2012-2013, 6,400 people slept rough in London at one point and about 2,300 in the rest of England. However, rough sleeping is only one measure of homelessness and there were also 43,000 people living in hostels and an unknown number in squats or crashing with friends. Despite serious efforts the problem is on the rise again.

Why do people become beggars? The reasons are complex and often hard to discover. Many people adopted that way of living because of misfortune, mental illness or an excessive fondness for alcohol; for a few, it was the result of family influence. Some were born to the life. Henry Mayhew met a man who had been forced by his mother to beg and who said, 'I never was anything else but a beggar. How could I? It was the trade I was brought up to. A man must follow his trade. No doubt I shall die a beggar and the parish will bury me'.

The Welsh poet W.H. Davies, who spent a number of years as a tramp or hobo in Britain and USA, was probably influenced in his choice of lifestyle by his uncle, who tramped around Wales selling laces and other knick-knacks and developed a profound objection to hard work. According to Davies, 'It has quite upset him to hear that I have degenerated into a worker; but he is pleased to know that it is mental work and that I never sweat or soil my hands'.

A few people became beggars because of misfortune and behavioural issues as young people. Mary Saxby, a famous eighteenth century wanderer, attributed her itinerant life to events in her childhood. Her mother died when she was young and her father went into the army. Mary was passed from relative to relative, never staying long, 'in consequence of my own perverse temper'. Eventually her father returned with a new wife of whom Mary disapproved and, one day, being sent on an errand by her father, she lost the shilling he had given her and, fearing punishment, ran away. When George Atkins Brine, one of the men who claimed to be 'King of the Beggars', was a youth he was frequently in trouble with the law for minor offences and served many short periods in gaol. He was eventually threatened with the cat-o'-nine-tails if he reoffended and to avoid a beating, he took to the road.

Others were driven to vagrancy by mental illness. In 1905, a Salvation Army survey of London casual wards estimated that 82 per cent of inmates were mentally fit, and the remainder had some psychiatric issues. By 1929, it was estimated that 5.4 per cent of vagrants had senile dementia, while 5.7 per cent had psychoneurotic illnesses, many of which dated back to shell shock in the Great War. Today, almost half have mental health needs. Centrepoint, the charity for young homeless has identified the reasons why young people become homeless; like Mary Saxby, many left home because of arguments and relationship breakdown, while others grew up in poverty and workless households. Others had mental health problems and issues with substance abuse, while some engaged in destructive or anti-social behaviour.

Some people started on the road in a genuine effort to find work, but then fell into the begging life. W.H. Davies described how a man might begin tramping from town to town hoping to find employment, but would become discouraged and after a time find that it was not so hard to beg to get enough money for food and lodgings. Then it would not be long before he is heard to say in a lodging house kitchen while he is drinking hot tea and eating fresh toast 'Who's looking for work, eh? Not me'.

For many people, the dividing line between begging and employment was very thin. In the eighteenth century, many ways of earning a living, notably being a shoe black or a crossing sweeper, were little more than disguised forms of begging, while char ladies often got paid in food as a reward for helping richer servants.

Some beggars were simply work-shy and preferred an easy life. In 1820, Pierce Egan produced a magazine called *Life in London*, featuring Jerry Hawthorn and Corinthian Tom (who were the inspiration for the cartoon characters Tom and Jerry). One of his stories was about a tinsmith who had bought some genteel clothes and a brush and had become a crossing sweeper. He was arrested for his saucy behaviour to a lady who would not give him money. He asked his fellow prisoners 'Who would work hard for a few shillings per day when, with only a broom in his hand, a polite bow and a genteel appearance at the corner of any of the Squares, the ladies could be gammoned out of pounds per week'.

W.H. Davies described how, while in America, he fell under the influence of a notorious beggar called Brum who was so idle that he would rather beg for a new shirt than sew a button on an old one. Under Brum's teaching, Davies became 'a lazy wretch with little inclination for work'. Brum once got into trouble with another vagrant at a campsite because he had managed to beg a good pair of trousers. The other man began by glaring hatefully at his trousers. It was only when Brum unloaded eight or nine parcels of food, which he had hidden in his clothes, that the other beggar came forward and said 'Excuse me boys for not giving you a more hearty welcome, but really' – glancing again at my companion's trousers – 'I thought you were working men, but now I see that you are true beggars'.

For others, the call of the road was the attraction. Beggars' literature is full of examples of people who have given up perfectly reasonable jobs because they could not resist the vagabond life. After Mary Saxby left home, she was fortunate enough to meet a motherly woman who took care of her, but her 'proud, imperious temper', forced her to run away and begin life as a singer of street ballads. Even when she was older and had become an evangelical Christian, Mary Saxby could not resist the call of the road. She tramped around, tracts in hand, bent on converting sinners and wrote 'Many refreshing seasons I have enjoyed, with my bible in my hand, as I have walked from town to town'.

George Atkins Brine once found employment with a butcher. 'Had I stopped with the butcher, I might have gone on very well, for I was somewhat of a favourite with him. But the itching for a turn on the road came over me and go I must'. Later he got a job working on a wharf in Everton and worked all winter, but 'With the first buds of spring I was seized with an old tramp's longing for the freedom of the road, and one Monday morning, instead of going to work I crossed the ferry into Cheshire and started on my travels again'.

A tramp whom Mayhew met described how he had once worked for a gentleman as a servant, 'He was a very kind man; I had a good place, swell clothes and beef and beer as much as I liked, but I couldn't stand the life and I run away'.

In later life, when he was a successful poet W.H. Davies wrote two books *Autobiography of a Super Tramp* and *Beggars* about his life as a tramp or hobo in Britain and North America, sometimes taking casual work, other times begging for food and money. In *Beggars* he explained why he loved the life of a tramp:

When I consider what pleasure it gives me to lie abed in the mornings at my own sweet will, I cannot help but feel pity for the great majority who must needs rise to answer the demands of civilization. Of course, I could not myself be so independent if I were not contented with very little and did not prefer freedom to fine clothes and furniture and the luxuries of food. Honestly if I had not been cursed with ambition to excel in litera-ture, I would have remained a beggar to the end of my days; to winter in Baltimore and spend my summer months in travelling through the green country, with short stops here and there in cities and large towns.

Beggars often found it hard to hold on to money. When W.H. Davies lost part of his leg in an accident in Ontario, kind townspeople had a collection for him and he was able to return to Newport with £120. He rapidly spent half of it drinking with his friends and had to flee to London to live in hostels in order to retain the little he had left. Brine managed to save £10 and went to Liverpool with the intention of going to America. But he went on the spree and woke up the next morning in a police cell with a splitting headache and all his money gone.

Drink is one of the major contributing factors behind beggary. Brine admitted that throughout his life drink had always been his curse and his biography is full of the scrapes he got into when drunk, including the tragic night when he and Bradford Dick were going home drunk, fell into the canal and Dick was drowned. In 1899, it was estimated that 90 per cent of all vagrancy was due to drink. W.H. Davies put his problems with drink down to the fact that he was brought up in a pub and given mulled beer at bed-time instead of cocoa.

Not all drunken beggars took themselves seriously. In the eight-eenth century, Richard Steele came upon a beggar who told him that he was very poor and would die in the street of lack of drink, unless Steele immediately gave him sixpence so that he could go into the nearest alehouse and save his life. He claimed that all his family had died of thirst. Mayhew told the story of an elderly woman who would fall down and appear to have a fit; this usually happened near to the door of an alehouse, when a well-dressed man was passing with a lady on his arm. The only word the woman ever spoke during one of her 'fits' was 'Brandy', in case that remedy did not suggest itself to those who came to her aid. According to a policeman, she sometimes had so many fits in the day that she was found drunk in the gutter from the effect of repeated restoratives.

Some people were so desperate for a glass of strong drink that, according to Mayhew, they would throw themselves into the Serpen-tine in the hope of being rescued and taken to the hut belonging to the Humane Society, where they were revived with brandy. Eventually the staff of the Humane Society began to recognize one regular offender and refused to rescue him. He soon found his way out of the water once he saw that his dodge had been detected.

Some beggars are honest in asking for what they want – a colleague was approached by a beggar in Covent Garden who told her that he wanted money for alcohol and drugs. I once saw an elderly tramp in Notting Hill who was slumped outside a chemist's shop, drinking wine from a Starbucks cup. The bottle he was clutching was not some supermarket own-brand Moroccan red, but a rather decent bottle of claret.

The major centre of begging in London between 1860 and 1930 was not the claret-drinking streets of Notting Hill, but a few miles to the east along the Embankment. Here beggars could sleep on the benches along the river, shelter from the rain and snow under the bridges and have a chance to beg in the West End, or scrounge food from generous cooks and waiters in the hotels and restaurants along the Strand. In 1890, William Booth found 368 people sleeping between Westminster and Blackfriars and by 1909 there were between 500 and 1,200 a night. Such a concentration of beggars attracted a large number of charities – one was giving away 800 meals a day. Some organizations were not very discriminating in their giving: John Burns, the President of the Local Government Board, was offered a free meal by a charity worker when he paid a visit.

In 1912 the Night Office was set up on Waterloo Pier by the London County Council to coordinate the charities' work. Staff directed 'help-able' people to night shelters run by charities, while regulars were sent to casual wards. As a result, the number of rough sleepers in the area fell from 983 a night in February 1912 to 491 in February 1913 and less than 100 by 1930.

Since at least the fourteenth century, governments have been con-cerned about vagabonds and sturdy beggars; men and women who were fit enough to work, but, preferred a life of wandering and of getting money by begging and trickery instead. The sixteenth century was a period of social disruption, with inflation, changes in agriculture and frequent problems caused by discharged soldiers and sailors wandering the country. An Act of 1531 proclaimed that persons who were able bodied, had no land or craft and could give no reckoning as to how they could get their living were to be whipped and sent back to the place where they were born or had last lived for three years and then put to work.

In 1572, Queen Elizabeth's Parliament passed an Act that attempted to define who these sturdy beggars were. Not only were they able-bodied people who did not have a trade and who could not explain how they could make a living, but they also included a whole host of others – fortune tellers (people with a knowledge of physiognomy or palmistry or other abused sciences), fencers, people who kept bears for entertainment, jugglers and minstrels, as well as unlicensed pedlars and tinkers. Such people were to be burned through the ear and put to work.

From the seventeenth century, a general pattern for dealing with beggars had emerged. The genuinely sick or old were cared for by their parishes, while some able-bodied people were encouraged to earn an honest living as licensed pedlars and tinkers. In addition people who were genuinely deserving, could be issued with licences allowing them to beg.

Until the early nineteenth century, the government recognized three categories of sturdy beggars: firstly idle and disorderly people who remained within their own parishes; these could be jailed for a month. Secondly rogues and vagabonds; these were mainly beggars who had wandered outside their own parishes, but the category also included a whole range of travelling entertainers and fortune-tellers, who could be whipped, jailed and returned to their own parishes. Finally, there were incorrigible rogues who persisted in their anti-social behaviour. They could be whipped, imprisoned for two years and either impressed into the army or transported.

The system was widely abused. Vagrants were given passes to enable them to claim relief from parishes on their route home. Often, the parishes contracted out the responsibility of transporting vagrants to private enterprise 'pass masters'. A pass was a valuable object guaranteeing the holder the ability to move from place to place and some form of support on their way and so these were often forged. In 1784 Eleanor Clarke was arrested in the parish of St Andrew, Holborn for 'wandering abroad with sundry passes under different characters and descriptions'.

In practice, the law was not always well enforced. Part of the problem was that local constables were rewarded for arresting vagrants but not for securing convictions. So there were many cases in which a police constable would arrest an offender, claim the reward and then not turn up at the trial. Therefore, in 1824 the law was changed. Rewards to the police for arresting vagrants were abolished, while only incorrigible ones could be whipped and rough sleeping was made a crime. The Act was considered to be harsh and there was a genuine dislike of the idea of the police arresting vagrants. Magistrates were very reluctant to convict – in 1852 there were 3,708 prosecutions of vagrants by the Metropolitan Police, but nearly half of these resulted in acquittals. In 1910, Horatio Bottomley MP asked the Home Secretary whether the poor wretches sleeping on the Embankment were doing more harm than ministers sleeping on the benches in the House.

The punitive approach to rough sleeping came to an end in the 1930s. In 1933, an unemployed war veteran, John Thomas Parker, was arrested near Birmingham and jailed for sleeping rough. He was an unruly individual and received three days' solitary imprisonment. He then either fell or threw himself down a flight of stairs and died. This resulted in a public scandal. In 1935 a new Act meant that rough sleeping was no longer an offence, unless the person had been directed to a shelter, or if they had caused damage or were a danger to public health.

Since the Elizabethan period there has been a popular fascination with low life and authors have catered for this by producing books, originally called 'Rogue Literature', describing the lives of criminals and beggars and allegedly revealing the secrets of the underworld. There were a number of writers of rogue literature in the late sixteenth and early seventeenth centuries, including Luke Hutton, who produced *The Black Dog of Newgate*, and Thomas Dekker, who wrote the wonderfully titled *Bellman of London* and *Lanthorne and Candlelight*. Dekker said they were written 'to shorten the lives of long winter nights that lie watching in the dark for us'. However, they do give us an insight into a world of crime and vagrancy that would otherwise be invisible.

One of the earliest and most influential writers of rogue literature was Thomas Harman who, in 1566 published *A Caveat for Common Cursitors, Vulgarly Called Vagabonds*. At some time Harman had been a magistrate, but he became unwell and later spent most of his time at home at Crayford in Kent, where he interviewed those beggars travelling along Watling Street who called at his house. Using 'fair flattering words, money and good cheer', he discovered their histories. Many of the stories he tells can be verified from other sources.

Harman became obsessed with sturdy beggars. He once rode into Dartford and came upon a 'Dummerer' (a deaf and dumb beggar). Harman examined the man's licence and suspected it was a forgery –

it had a seal that Harman recognized as fraudulent. When the beggar arrived in Crayford, Harman and a surgeon examined him. The surgeon opened his mouth and they could only see half his tongue. Suspecting a trick, he put his finger in the man's mouth and pulled his tongue out. The man had a whole tongue but still would not speak, so Harman and the surgeon had him hanged by his wrists from a beam. Eventually the man cried out because of the pain and begged to be let down. Harman confiscated the man's money, which was given to the poor, and sent him off to be whipped at the pillory.

On another occasion, Harman was in London when he saw a young man whom he described as a counterfeit crank, or someone pretending to have epilepsy. He was almost naked, with his head wrapped in a cloth and covered in blood and dirt. As Harman said, the sight was monstrous and terrible. He spoke to the beggar, one Nicholas Jennings from Leicester. Jennings claimed he had the falling sickness (that is epilepsy) and that he had been in Bethlem Hospital (popularly known as Bedlam).

Harman became suspicious and sent a servant to Bethlem to check him out. The hospital keeper had never heard of the man. So Harman borrowed two young employees from a printer friend and asked them to follow Jennings. They watched him begging all day and saw him collect a large amount of money. He had a short break in the middle of the day when he renewed his disguise of mud and blood. The blood came from a bladder he was carrying. Toward evening, he took a boat across the Thames to Newington. They followed him, eventually sending for the local constable, who arrested Jennings. When Jennings was stripped and searched, he was found to be carrying over 13 shillings (the equivalent of a week's wages for a labourer).

Jennings escaped, however, by tricking the constable's wife and fleed stark naked. Harman subsequently persuaded the parish officials to give the money taken from Jennings to the local poor. Jennings resumed his career as a beggar, at first as a sailor whose ship had been lost at sea and later as a hatter who had come to London looking for work. Unfortunately, he tried to beg from Harman's printer, who recognized him and had him arrested. It turned out that Jennings (whose real name was Nicholas Blunt) had a nice house in Newington and a wife. He was imprisoned in the Bridewell, whipped at a cart's tail through the streets and then dressed in both his respectable clothes and the clothes he used for begging and put in the pillory at Cheapside.

Many beggars' tricks continued to be in use for hundreds of years. Nicholas Jennings's impersonation of epilepsy was a popular dodge with sturdy beggars. In the nineteenth century, George Atkins Brine horrified the people of Northampton by pretending to have a fit. He made it all the more realistic by pricking his gums with a pin to draw blood and also putting some soap in his mouth to create froth. Once he had been revived with brandy, he told the crowd who had gathered that he was trying to raise money to get to Dorset and a collection was held for him.

The dodge continued to be used as late as 1900, when the Mendicity Society arrested a notorious trickster known as the Soap Fit King in East Dulwich. However, as Mayhew said, simulating fits requires good acting ability – agitating the muscles, turning up the whites of the eyes, having a pallid face and a rigid mouth and jaw. Other dodges involved creating artificial wounds, which could be displayed to horrific effect. In the seventeenth century, rogues called palliards, clapper-dudgeons or washmen used spearwort to cause a blister and then added ratsbane (arsenic) to make it look worse. These practices continued until the nineteenth century, although by then imitation wounds were created by applying a thick layer of soap and dropping vinegar on to it.

Some forms of physical disability could easily be counterfeited. George Atkins Brine had a clear understanding of the psychology behind begging in this way. He wrote:

Imposture like every other trade, requires for thorough success a long apprenticeship and a keen observance of the foibles and weaknesses of human nature. To enlist sympathy the beggar must appeal to the eye and the ear. It is no use looking jovial and happy, and then complain of being ill and miserable; and there are few natures so hardened as not to be stirred by an appeal of simulated sickness and sorrow.

Being dressed in rags helped; Jonathan Swift said of beggars 'neither do they much regard clothes unless to sell them; for their rags are part of their tools with which they work'.

Although Brine could give good advice he was pretty hopeless as a beggar himself. While tramping through Wales he pretended to be dumb, but a policeman visited the lodging house he was staying in and began searching his coat. Brine protested and ended up in Usk gaol for three months.

The practice of pretending to be disabled continued up to the nineteenth century. Mayhew has a story about a blind beggar whose dog carried a little basket into which people could put money. Boys would try to steal money from the basket, but when they approached the dog, the blind man would run at them with his stick. On another occasion, Mayhew met a man who had lost an arm in a poaching accident. He told Mayhew 'The loss of my arm, sir, was the best thing as ever happened to me; I turn out with it on all sorts of lays and it's as good as a pension'.

It was also easy to demonstrate the symptoms of various forms of mental illness and the writers of rogue literature often refer to 'Abraham Men'. These were people who pretended to be insane; some claimed they were former patients of Bedlam Hospital and often referred to themselves as 'Tom O'Bedlam'. One famous Abraham Man was called Stradling; he claimed to be the former servant of Lord Stourton and to have been driven mad with grief and fear when his master was executed for murder in 1556. He demonstrated a great skill at shaking like a leaf when seeking alms.

The most famous Tom O'Bedlam was Edgar in *King Lear* and it may well be that in his rantings we hear the genuine voice of the Abraham Man. Harman explained that 'Some of these be merry and very pleasant; they will dance and sing; some others be as cold and reasonable to talk withal ... if they espy small company within they will with fierce countenance demand somewhat. Where for fear the maids will give them largely to be rid of them'.

One way in which beggars throughout the ages have tried to raise money is to pretend to be shipwrecked sailors. In the sixteenth century these were known as 'Whipjacks' or 'Freshwater Mariners'. Good quality faked licences allowing distressed mariners to beg were on sale in Portsmouth and the fake sailors took good care to beg in counties, such as Hertfordshire and Oxfordshire, well away from the sea. According to Harman, most of the ships of these freshwater mariners were sunk on Salisbury Plain.

Some 300 years later, in 1862 Henry Mayhew described very similar categories of beggars. He talked about naval beggars whom he described as 'Turnpike Sailors'. These dressed in the sort of naval costumes pictured on the covers of popular song sheets – bare feet, Guernsey shirt, black silk handkerchiefs, gold earrings and tattoos of anchors and mermaids. Normally such men were found in inland towns, a long way from the haunts of real sailors. George Atkins Brine also tried the old sailor trick. He was in Bridlington when a ship, the *Yorkshire Lass* was wrecked nearby. He found the body of a sailor and stole his clothes and papers. Unfortunately, the first house he visited was in Beverley and turned out to be the home of a retired sea captain, who instantly knew him as a fraud and gave him a sound beating. Brine then went to Hull, where he was arrested and searched and the sailor's papers were found in his pocket. He was sentenced to three months in York Castle.

False sailors also had their military equivalent. In the sixteenth century, old soldiers and people pretending to have served in the wars were referred to as 'rufflers'. They frequently displayed old wounds they had acquired in drunken brawls. By the nineteenth century, they were known as 'Street Campaigners'; some of these were genuine old soldiers who were unable to find work; others were men who had been dismissed from the army for misconduct, although most were purely impostors who made the most of missing or damaged limbs by acquiring military costumes and standing to attention on crowded streets with a placard round their necks setting out their hardships.

W.H. Davies knew a man who made a living by pretending to be a Boer War veteran. He travelled through Gloucestershire and Monmouthshire, calling on the homes of retired officers and producing forged letters from men he claimed to have served under. He did so well that he no longer called at small houses for pennies, but at large ones for silver.

The periods immediately after wars saw large numbers of genuine soldiers on the roads and after the First World War, 80 per cent of tramps were ex-soldiers. In 1932 it was claimed that in Kettering Casual Ward there were two men with Military Crosses, 44 with Military Medals and one with a Croix de Guerre. In addition there were fraudulent soldiers and even a bogus choir of ex-servicemen songsters in the 1920s.

In 1561, John Awdeley published his *Fraternitie of Vagabonds*. He described a trick carried out by men whom he called 'Ringfallers'. They had a cheap gilt copper ring which they would drop in the street in front of a simple countryman. They made a big show of picking it up and offering the victim a half-share; they then offered to buy the victim's half-share from him, but eventually persuaded him to pay them for their share; leaving them with cash and the victim with a ring of little value. Centuries later, in March 2013, the *Evening Standard* reported the latest scam in London. Criminal gangs from Eastern

Europe are fooling people into handing over cash for worthless metal rings. They drop a gold-coloured ring next to an unsuspecting passer-by, they then point out the ring to the intended victim and ask if it belongs to them. When the victim says 'no' the trickster offers to sell it to them for anything up to £20.

By the nineteenth century, new tricks had emerged. One of these was the clergyman dodge. George Atkins Brine used it several times, but, like many of his tricks, it went badly wrong. At first he was a successful mock-cleric, but then he did some street preaching in Liverpool where he was arrested. Nothing daunted, he went to Manchester and tried again. This time the outcome was three months in prison. On release, he begged a suit of clothes from the chaplain and tried to pass as a clergyman-tutor who was temporarily in distress. This worked well until he reached Thetford, where he was arrested and spent another month in prison.

Later, after a couple more stretches in prison, he was in Middles-brough where he met a Welshman and persuaded him that he was an experienced Methodist lay preacher. The local chapel had just lost their minister and Brine offered to preach a sermon, which he did very successfully. The next night he gave a lecture on the People's Charter. Unfortunately, however, then he managed to self-destruct. He ran into an old tramp called 'Barmy Joe' at his lodging house and spent the evening drinking some stolen cognac with Joe and a couple of other travellers. A policeman visited the lodging house late that evening and saw Brine carousing. The next day he received a stern visit from his friend at the chapel. The policeman was one of the congregation and was shocked to find the preacher spending the night drinking with tramps. That was the end of Brine's career in holy orders.

Closely associated with the clergyman dodge were the respectable tradesmen who had fallen on hard times. Mayhew called them ashamed beggars – men who dressed like tradesmen, wearing spotless white aprons and carrying notices telling of their misfortunes; often they sold matches, notepaper, envelopes and sealing wax. Dickens met such a man while out walking in Kent. He claimed to have been a law stationer who had lost his business through illness in the family and the treachery of his brother-in-law, for whom he had acted as surety. He was on his way to Dover to seek help from a relative. He tried to sell Dickens a cheap comb.

Many beggars pretended to be pedlars and carried stocks of small goods – pins, needles, matches, laces etc for sale. This was a legal dodge because, while it was illegal to be a vagrant, it was possible to obtain a pedlar's licence and then to travel the country legally. A licence was not needed to sell perishable goods and so some beggars who could not afford a peddler's licence carried packets of finkum (lavender), which they would produce if stopped by the police.

Of course, beggars were not interested in selling their small stock of materials; they really wanted people to give them money. W.H. Davies said that 'it is not sufficient to sell a farthing pair of laces for a penny but to tell such a pitiful story that the buyer out of pity for misfortunes returns the laces after paying for them and occasionally adds a piece of cake to her kindness'. Mayhew said that the price of most things sold by beggars was much cheaper in the shops and so people only bought them out of charity.

One step above the fraudulent beggars were the street entertainers, who at least offered something in return for a few pennies. The most common seem to have been singers referred to as 'griddlers' or 'grizzlers'. Some of these, known to as 'chaunters', also sold the words of the ballads they were singing. According to W.H. Davies, griddlers with poor voices did better than those with good ones. All that was needed was for a griddler to choose a simple, well-known hymn and sing it in a cracked or shaky voice and a sympathetic audience would shower him or her with coppers.

Some singers were in league with pickpockets. In 1592, Henry Chettle described how a man called Barnes taught his sons to sing bawdy songs and while people listened they found that their knives and purses had been stolen. A similar story was told in 1597 in a pamphlet called 'Mihil Mumchance: his discoverie of the art of cheating in false dyce play', which concerned a juggler who climbed a steeple to distract people while a cutpurse got to work below.

One of the interesting questions about tramps is the extent to which they were part of organized groups or were solitary individuals. The authors of the rogue literature pamphlets liked to suggest that there was a society of beggars. They talked a lot about 'Upright Men' who had authority over other beggars and the power to initiate them into the fellowship of rogues by pouring beer over their heads. There were some examples of organized crime in the sixteenth century. In 1585, the City Recorder of London wrote to Lord Burghley about a school for pickpockets he had found in Billingsgate – a pocket and a purse were hung with bells and the trainees had to remove the money without making any noise.

In the early nineteenth century, Tom and Jerry visited a club for beggars, called the Cadgers, where they saw disabled men throw away their crutches and dance, blind beggars able to see and half-starved ones eating the finest delicacies. A few years later, Mayhew the journalist and social investigator met a beggar who had lived in Pye Street, Westminster, in two houses owned by one 'Copenhagen Jack', who ran teams of beggars with different specialities – disabled, those who pretended to be blind and those who gave the impression of having palsy. Later he lived in a house in St Giles with about a hundred beggars. In the 1920s, Jim Sullivan a lodging-housekeeper sent beggars out to organized pitches; some were unemployed miners, others were ex-servicemen and yet others sold matches. His commission was 10 per cent of their takings and he employed crows (watchers) to protect the pitches and see that he got his correct pay off.

However, the few autobiographies of vagrants show rather a different view. Most were not members of organized gangs – they lived rather solitary lives, finding companionship for a few days and then going off on their own. Undoubtedly, much of the literature about gangs of beggars is simply designed to frighten and thrill readers, in the same way that we are frightened and thrilled by the idea of organized crime.

One thing that set sturdy beggars, rogues and vagabonds apart and perhaps gave them an appearance of being part of organized gangs was their use of special words and expressions. The use of a rogue's language was known as early as the fifteenth century, but became famous in the sixteenth century with the popularity of rogue literature. Thomas Harman described it as 'the lewd lousy language of these lewtering Lusks and lazy Lorels'. Many of these Tudor terms are unfamiliar and strange to us, but are graphic in their descriptive power – 'prancer' for horse, 'glimmer' for fire, 'glaziers' for eyes, 'stamps' for legs, 'lightmans' for daytime and 'darkmans' for the night. A couple of words have passed into popular usage – 'bouse' is now booze, while 'bung' which is the canting term for a purse, now means a bribe.

More modern writers listed canting terms familiar to us: Orwell mentions 'peter' for a safe, 'boozer' for pub, 'knock off' for steal and 'clodhopper', which in his day meant dancer. But both he and Davies describe cant words which have fallen out of use – 'moocher' for beggar (the word mooch is still used to describe an aimless stroll), 'mugfaker' for photographer, 'scrand' meaning food and 'skimish' for drink. Anyone who has watched *The Wire* on television will have an idea of how impenetrable criminal slang can be and the language used by beggars in early twentieth century England may have been as difficult for an outsider to understand.

In the nineteenth century, black beggars were part of the London scene and when Tom and Jerry visited the beggar's club the music was provided by a black one-legged fiddler called Billy Waters. George Atkins Brine spent some time travelling with a black American woman called Linda, whom he persuaded to pretend to be a runaway slave. He would give a lecture and Linda would sing slavery songs. Dickens spoke of the escaped slave 'whose back was marked as with scars from the leathern and wiry claws of the slave driver's cat'. In the 1870s, Joe Johnson, a black former merchant seaman, was famous for begging in London wearing a model of the ship *Nelson* on his head and bobbing up and down to give the impression of a ship at sea.

In the sixteenth century, women beggars too, were common. Thomas Harman spoke to an old man who remembered an incident in 1521 when a feast was prepared in a barn to celebrate a funeral. A crowd of beggars came and the old man counted seven score (140) men, every one with a woman, 'except it were two women that lay alone together for some special cause'. Harman knew of a barn near Blackheath where 40 beggars lay with their women. He described the various categories of women beggars – 'demanders for glimmer', who claimed that their houses had been burned down; 'bawdy baskets', who carried baskets full of trinkets which they would sell to maid servants when their mistresses were out of the house; they also had a line in clothes stealing and prostitution. Then there were 'walking morts', who claimed that their husbands had died at Newhaven or Ireland or elsewhere in the service of the prince. Finally were the 'autem morts', married women who stole clothes off hedges and sent their children into houses to steal.

In the eighteenth century, female beggars outnumbered their male counterparts. Between 1738 and 1742, just over half the beggars who were arrested for begging and loitering were adult women, 8 per cent were children and 40 per cent were adult men. In 1796, Matthew Martin surveyed street beggars in London. Of the 2,000 adults he saw, only 192 were men; of the women, 127 were single, 1,100 were married and 58 were widowed; 240 of the women were either wives or widows of soldiers and sailors.

But this would change: between 1833 and 1843 only a quarter of vagrants taken into custody by the Metropolitan Police were female, while by 1900 they had pretty much disappeared. In 1904 the London County Council did a survey of homeless people, finding that 2,510 men were sleeping rough but only 220 women.

George Orwell, who wrote about his experiences on the road in the 1930s, said that 'a tramp is celibate from the moment when he takes to the road. He is absolutely without hope of getting a wife, a mistress or any kind of woman'. This decline in the numbers of women vagrants has never been satisfactorily explained. One possible reason is that there was a degree of miscounting – women who were living as prostitutes may have been included in the figures for beggars in the eighteenth century and excluded in the nineteenth.

However, the reduction in the number of women beggars seems too great to be accounted for by statistical error. Broadly, in the sixteenth century most male beggars had female partners, yet by the twentieth century, beggars were largely celibate. The change seems to have occurred in the nineteenth century and two factors may account for it. First, there seems to have been a growth in the number of opportunities for women in domestic service. The figures are complex and difficult to interpret but, after a tax on male servants was introduced, domestic service gradually switched from a male occupation to a female one over the course of the eighteenth and early nineteenth centuries.

More importantly, for women who might have otherwise have become beggars, the cost of employing live-in servants rose over this period and many middle class homes seem to have employed increasing numbers of char-women and others to supplement their live-in servants. Secondly and more certainly, between 1889 and 1908 a series of Acts of Parliament made it illegal for parents to cause their children to beg or to entertain as a form of begging. Clearly this legislation made it harder for women with children to pursue a life on the road.

Children were a key part of begging culture until the late nineteenth century. In the seventeenth century the sons and daughters of vagrants were referred to as 'Kinchin Cos' and 'Kinchin Morts'. From that time onwards there were numbers of children sleeping rough in London. In the early seventeenth century several hundred were rounded up and sent as cheap labour to the colonies in Barbados and Virginia.

When Matthew Martin surveyed beggars in London in 1796, he found 3,096 children, as well as 2,000 adults. Some of these children slept under 'bulks', the heavy wooden shelves jutting out from the fronts of shops, while others slept in Fleet or Leadenhall Markets which provided the possibility of free leftover food. When Mary Saxby first ran away from home, she crept under bulks and at daybreak went into the markets to pick up rotten apples and cabbage stalks.

There was also a gang of London street children called the Black Guard, who spent their nights among the glass factories of the Minories. These were warm places to sleep, with the added possibility of getting work running errands. Like many aspects of the lives of beggars, the stories of the Black Guard are a strange mixture of fact and fiction. They were the subject of scare stories in newspapers and Daniel Defoe wrote about them in his 1722 novel *Colonel Jack*.

Beggars would rent children out by the day – a man or woman with a child was always a more likely object for pity. In 1744, the anonymous author of *A Trip from St James's to the Royal Exchange* described how he had visited the Infant Exchange in St Giles, where beggars could hire out infants for the day. When Tom and Jerry visited the beggars' club, they talked about a poor married woman with twins who was in distress because her husband had been sent to sea. In reality, she was a single woman who had hired the children.

Bampfylde Moore Carew was probably the most unscrupulous exploiter of children – he used to pretend that his wife had been drowned in a shipwreck off the Welsh coast and would carry his little daughter on his back when out begging. He had taught her to say 'drowned in a boat' when anyone asked her where her mother was. W.H. Davies talked about an incident where the wife of a knife grinder hired out her seven-year-old daughter to a ballad singer: 'you can have the kid all day, it's not the first time, by a long way for Mary Ann to be used by griddlers, and she knows as well as you what's wanted of her'.

There were still large numbers of street children by the middle of the nineteenth century. Anthony Ashley Cooper, in 1848, described how an army of 'street Arabs' slept in arches, porticoes, sheds, carts, saw-pits, outhouses and even the iron roller in Regent's Park. By the late nineteenth century their numbers were declining rapidly. This was partly due to charities such as Dr Barnado's Homes, which was set up in 1866 to rescue children from the street, and, as mentioned earlier, to legislative changes which made it an offence for parents to cause their children to beg or to wander from place to place with a child. In the late 1850s it was estimated that there were 33,000 tramps in England and Wales: nearly a quarter of whom were children. By 1904, a survey of people sleeping in casual wards showed that only 2 per cent were children.

Casual wards were part of a network of places where tramps could find a place to sleep. Known as 'Spikes', these were part of the workhouse. They provided the roughest and most basic accommodation for those on the move – both vagrants and job seekers. They often only had straw for bedding and a meal of bread and gruel. New arrivals had their clothes heated in a stove to kill vermin and had to work for two hours each morning, breaking rocks or picking oakum (picking pieces of rope into its constituent fibres). Vagrants were not allowed to spend two consecutive nights in a ward or more than two nights a month in any one ward. This was a well-meaning piece of legislation designed to reduce vagrancy, but it had the opposite effect, creating a class of 'roundsmen'; tramps who would move from one casual ward to another.

If they were in funds, beggars much preferred the common lodging house or doss house. These offered very basic accommodation and were often cramped, insanitary and fairly horrendous. From 1851 local authorities began to regulate and inspect such institutions and conditions slowly improved. A few local authorities, notably Huddersfield and the London County Council, built municipal lodging houses; Bruce House in Covent Garden was the most famous of these.

In the nineteenth century, charities also began to provide accommodation for vagrants, starting with the Liverpool Night Asylum and the Houseless Poor Asylum in Cripplegate, London. But the most important charities were the Salvation Army and the Rowton Houses built by the philanthropist, Lord Rowton as accommodation for working men. Salvation Army hostels were mostly clean, but very closely regulated, with an air of religiosity that the inmates hated and, according to W.H. Davies, incredibly crowded – 'a row of fifteen or twenty beds would be so close together that they might be called one bed'.

Better value were the Rowton Houses, which cost a little more, but were very clean and provided lodgers with their own cubicles, however, they also had strict rules; cooking and card playing were not allowed. W.H. Davies lived in one for two years when he was beginning his career as a writer – he was impressed by their cleanliness and comparatively lavish facilities, consisting of dining rooms, sitting rooms, library, baths, etc. George Orwell, like most vagrants and beggars, preferred the common lodging house; although they were stuffy, noisy, dirty and uncomfortable, they had none of the rules and regulations of the charitable institutions and with their laissez-faire atmospheres and warm home-like kitchens, some sort of social life was possible.

Outside the big cities a number of ancient charities provided overnight accommodation or food and drink for those on the road. George Atkins Brine mentions such houses at Oxford, Cambridge, Bath, Norwich, Hastings and Rochester. The most famous of these is the Hospital of St Cross in Winchester, which provided a horn of ale and a morsel of bread to wayfarers from the end of the twelfth century.

In Rochester there was the House of the Six Poor Travellers. Over the door is an inscription which reads 'Richard Watts, by his will dated 16 August 1579, founded this charity for Six Poor Travellers who not being rogues or proctors may receive gratis one night's lodging, food, entertainment and four pence each'. Watts was a local gentleman, who served as a Member of Parliament and had been selected by Queen Elizabeth I to oversee the building of nearby Upnor Castle.

The charity had strict rules as to who could spend the night. Visitors could not be rogues, nor could they be proctors. Proctors were also sometimes known as fraters and were people licensed by the crown to collect money on behalf of hospitals or other religious institutions. For example, Robert ap Thomas ap Evans was licensed by Queen Elizabeth I to beg throughout Wales for the hospital of Our Lady of Bethlehem, as well as for various other charitable purposes.

People desiring a bed had to obtain a ticket from an official; up to 1880 these were issued at the local police station, but after that date poor travellers had to report to the local public baths (which had also been built by the charity). There were usually more applicants than places, so the trustees tried to make sure that the accommodation was provided to genuine travellers and not to beggars.

They were not always very successful. When Henry William Lucy, a journalist, was trying to spend a night in the house, he was questioned closely. He gave his occupation as paper stainer, and a policeman examined his hands to ensure that he was a genuine worker and not a tramp. He claims to have been successfully admitted. George Atkins Brine also visited and, since he was a tramp, he had to borrow some tools to make him look like a moulder. Brine believed that nine out of ten people who stayed in the house were impostors – tramps rather than genuine workers.

The poor travellers were given a meal of a half a pound of meat, a pound of bread and half a pint of porter. A good fire was provided from October 18 to March 10. Most importantly, the rules of the charity required the warden of the house to keep it clean and to treat the travellers courteously. The surviving accounts of people who stayed there give it good marks for both courtesy and cleanliness.

The House of the Six Poor Travellers closed in 1940 because of wartime restrictions on travel in the Medway area – it is close to the major naval dockyard at Chatham and there were concerns about possible sabotage by enemy agents. The house is now an almshouse and includes a small museum.

*   *   *

Perhaps the most famous of all beggars was Bampfylde Moore Carew (1693–1759), a notorious con artist, rogue, vagabond and imposter, who claimed to be 'king of the beggars'. We know about him because towards the end of his life he dictated an autobiography, which is a classic of rogue literature and an eighteenth century equivalent of some of the great sixteenth century works in that genre. Carew's autobiography was published in different editions for over 100 years; the later versions were more fanciful and entertaining than the original text. On the title page he was described as 'the Noted Devonshire Stroller and Dogstealer'. There is little other evidence beyond Carew's own account and many of his stories are too fantastic to be true, but they do give us a general picture of the approaches taken by an eighteenth century beggar many of which are amazingly similar to modern tricks and rogueries.

Carew was a member of a long-established Devonshire family; his father was the Reverend Theodore Carew, rector of Bickleigh. His unusual names come from his two godfathers – Hugh Bampfylde and Major Moore. Doubtless his father, who had several other children to provide for, had great expectations of these two gentlemen. Carew was sent to Blundell's School in Tiverton, Devon, with the intention that he would eventually become a clergyman. The school kept a pack of hounds to provide sport for its pupils. Carew and some friends took the pack out to hunt deer and did so much damage to crops that the local farmers complained to the headmaster. Carew and his chums fled the school and went to a local alehouse, where they fell in with a group of gypsies. Carew joined the troupe and travelled widely around the country making a living by playing tricks on the wealthy.

His first victim was a Madame Musgrove of Monkton, Devon. The innocent lady believed that there was a large treasure buried on her property and asked Carew's advice. Using what seems to have been folk-magic, he claimed that the treasure was under a laurel bush in her garden but that it would only be found on a day determined by her planet of fortune. She rewarded him with 20 guineas, but when the appointed day came neither the treasure, nor Carew, nor the 20 guineas could be found. Later he learned new folk magic skills, including the arts of curing madness in dogs and cattle.

Carew became a beggar, using his considerable talent for acting and dressing up to good advantage. First he pretended to be a shipwrecked sailor. According to his biography, he even went on a voyage to Newfoundland and back. The knowledge he acquired of the seaports of Canada on the voyage made him much more convincing as a beggar and he was even able to beg money from sea captains whom he convinced that he was a sailor on a ship wrecked on its way back from Newfoundland.

Later he pretended to be a farmer from the Isle of Sheppey whose farm had been flooded and who had a wife and seven children to support. As we saw in the chapter on begging letter writers, 'Sky farmers', who had lost their farms and who had wives and families to maintain, were a fixture among eighteenth century beggars. Next, like the Tom O'Bedlams of the sixteenth century, Carew would visit people's houses, dressed only in a blanket and act the part of a madman, offering to eat burning coal, dashing into walls, tearing the clothes that had been given to him. Eventually he would be given money to go away.

Carew was an expert in using real recent disasters as a way of gaining sympathy. In 1743 a great fire started in Crediton, Devon, completely destroying much of the town. Carew's response was to dress up as an elderly grandmother, borrow three young children and claim to be one of the victims of the fire in which the mother of the three children had died. One of the men who gave money to this elderly lady remarked that more money had been collected for Crediton than Crediton was worth.

Using disasters has long been a way for tricksters to raise money. Mayhew, writing in 1862, talks about 'blown up miners'; men who dressed like miners and pretended to have been injured or thrown out of work by a recent explosion in a pit. Although there were a few genuine cases, he believed that most of those whom he met in London came from Wentworth Street and Brick Lane in Whitechapel and had not been nearer to Yorkshire than Mile End.

One way to ensure credibility as a beggar, as we saw in the case of the begging letter writer, Alice Hammond, is to get the patronage of some wealthy individual. If you can point to a duke as your patron, it is much easier to secure the patronage of earls or barons. Carew managed to get an audience with the Duke of Bolton and persuaded him that he was the prodigal son of a respectable Devonshire family. The Duke provided him with a new suit of clothes and money. Once he had obtained the Duke's support, he was able to call on the mayor of Salisbury, the bishop and various other gentlemen, who were so impressed by the patronage of the duke that they funded him lavishly.

One of the main set pieces in the biography is Carew's account of the deathbed speech of Clause Patch, King of the Beggars. Like much of the book, this story is entirely fictitious; Patch is a fictional figure, who first appeared in the 1662, play, *Beggar's Bush*. Nevertheless, it contains some valuable psychological insights, which are still useful to anyone contemplating the career of sturdy beggar (or even internet fraudster). The mythical Patch said that there are two great passions that beggars can exploit – pity and vanity and that vanity is a far more powerful motivator than pity. Far more people give money to rid themselves of a beggar who is making a nuisance than do so out of charity and even more give as a public demonstration of their generosity than out of real compassion. Consequently, it is important to ask for money where many people can see it being given.

Patch also claimed that there was little profit in begging from the nobility, who have been made vain and insensitive by prosperity. Instead, it is better to get information about your neighbours and to exploit that. For example if a family has lost a son, pretend that your elder brother just lost one. If a woman has a sick husband, then offer to pray for him. If the husband dies, then get your sister to pretend that she has recently been left a widow with seven children. This method of getting very precise information about people and then using it to cheat them is used heavily on the internet and is referred to as 'spear phishing'.

Successful spear phishers assemble publicly available information from sites such as Google and LinkedIn to build up a picture of their target. They can then use this in various ways – they might, for example, discover that a person is interested in a particular make of car and use that information to send them carefully crafted emails which will include a link to a compromised website. Alternatively, they might use this knowledge to build up an online friendship with their target, who will eventually agree to become their friend on Facebook. Once they have access to confidential information on Facebook, they may find links to other sensitive material leaving the victim open to bribery or other crimes.

Soon after the fictional Patch died, Carew succeeded him as King of the Mendicants. Despite his new status, he continued his career of trickery. While in the parish of Fleet in Dorset, he heard of a ship stuck on some shoals and about to sink. He swam out to the ship and found one survivor clinging to the wreckage. Carew quizzed him about the name, cargo, destination and crew of the vessel before the wretch was washed away by a wave. Carew then struggled back to shore, where he was treated as a shipwrecked sailor and given clothes and money and a pass to travel to Bristol. Instead, he travelled to Devon, using the pass as a licence to beg from the local gentry.

He returned to Bristol and engaged in one of his most audacious scams – he remembered a man he had met in Newfoundland called Aaron Cook, whom he resembled. He decided to play the part of Cook's son and pretend that he had been in a ship which had been on its way to England but which sank off the coast of Ireland. Fortunately he had managed to get a passage for Bristol. He called on various ships' captains in Bristol who traded with Newfoundland and was able to persuade them that he really was the son of Aaron Cook their old friend. He seemed to have an intimate knowledge of the family and life of Aaron Cook, including a famous incident when the governor of Newfoundland had got a good beating at Aaron's house after saying that all the women in Newfoundland were whores. Naturally the captains did their best to help him out and send him on his way to Bridgewater, where he also called on other Newfoundland merchants who relieved him in his distress.

However, Carew soon met with disaster because one day he decided to visit an acquaintance, Mr Robert Incledon of Barnstaple. When he entered the house he was arrested by Justice Leithbridge, a sworn enemy of mendicants, who had a particular grievance against Carew because, while dressed as a disabled beggar, he had frightened the horse the Justice was riding over Hilton Bridge. The upshot was that Carew was transported to Maryland.

On his arrival he attempted to escape, but was captured and made to wear a heavy iron collar; he escaped again, and encountered some Native Americans, who removed his shackles. He was then said to have swum the Delaware River, after which he adopted the guise of a Quaker and made his way to Philadelphia, then to New York, where he embarked for England. On his way back to England he became concerned about being pressed into the Royal Navy and so demonstrated his beggar's skills by pricking his arms and chest with a needle, and then rubbing them with bay salt and gunpowder, which made it appear like smallpox. Eventually a Royal Navy vessel looking for men to press stopped the ship he was on. However, Carew was spared because the naval officer was terrified that he would spread the disease.

Once back in England, Carew resumed the career of a sturdy beggar taking on various disguises – a soap boiler whose factory had burned down, a poor Greek, a rat catcher and, once, he disguised himself as a 'Cousin Betty', a travelling prostitute, but most commonly he pretended to be a shipwrecked sailor. On one occasion, he met another beggar who was in the same line and they travelled together. Eventually it turned out that this beggar was really Lord Weymouth, who liked to amuse himself by dressing up in rags and begging from his neighbours.

Like so much about Carew's life, his final years are shrouded in mystery. According to one story, he had always maintained good relations with members of his family and a relative, Thomas Carew of Haccombe, offered to take care of him if he would give up the mendicant life. It is not clear if he accepted this offer; according to another version, he had a lottery win. Readers may prefer this alternative account:

> *Our hero returned home to the place of his nativity, but finding the air of the town not rightly to agree with him, and the death of some of his relations rendering his circumstances quite easy, he retired to the West Country, where he purchased a neat cottage, which he embellished in a handsome style, and lived in a manner becoming a good old English gentleman, respected by his neighbours, and beloved by the poor, to whom his doors were ever open. Here he died, full of years and honours, regretted by all.*

From the early nineteenth century, the number and character of beggars began to change and a vibrant part of the street scene began to disappear. Some leading writers demonstrated a remarkable sense of nostalgia for beggars. For Charles Lamb:

> *No corner of a street is complete without them. They are as indispensable as the ballad singer, and in their picturesque attire as ornamental as the*

signs of old London. They were the standing morals, emblems, mementos, dial mottos, the spital sermons, the books for children, the salutary checks and pauses to the high and rushing tide of greasy citizenry.

However, according to Lamb, they were threatened by social reforms which would compel them to work or provide relief for them. Consequently:

Scrips, wallets, bags – staves, dogs, and crutches – the whole mendicant fraternity with all their baggage are fast posting out of the purlieu of this eleventh persecution. From the crowded crossing, from the corners of streets and turnings of alleys, the parting Genius of Beggars is with sighing sent.

Dickens expressed similar views in an essay in *Household Words* in 1852. He lamented the disappearance of the characters who used to decorate London's streets. There was the Scotsman who dressed in four waistcoats and three coats but was without shoes or stockings. He supplemented his pension as a former soldier and managed to raise 30, 40 or 50 shillings a day by pure begging. Once when he was interrupted by a beadle trying to prevent him from begging, he invited him to a nearby public house where they dined on a pound of ham, half a pound of less savoury beef, a pint of rum and two tots of ale.

Then there was the man who dressed as a blinded sailor and was led by a dog, carrying his poor box in its mouth. When prosecuted, he claimed that it was the dog and not he who was begging. There was also a man with a 'valuable limp', which he stopped using when he retired into private life and had a second career as a first rate boxer. He remembered a time when London had its share of escaped slaves and also men who could use phrases of Latin and French when asking for alms.

Dickens recognized that there were a few old-style beggars left. There were old people who went from house to house selling matches, boot-laces and small memorandum books, using their sales as a cover for begging. There were elderly Irish beggars who sold match boxes and could beg eloquently. Finally, there were children, usually little girls, who bought small bunches of flowers at Covent Garden market and sold them in the streets; a way of life made famous by Bernard Shaw in *Pygmalion*. However, for the most part, the long-remembered public characters of his youth were as defunct as the stage coach.

Dickens put it down to Sir Robert Peel's new police, who had transformed life on the streets in London:

The New Policeman walks, with slow and measured steps, along dismantled or demolished streets, once the beggar's, the veritable beggar's hotel, his lavatory, his tiring-room, his harem. Streets, too which once rang with mendicant melody or malediction, are now purged and live cleanly.

Similar views were expressed by Lionel Rose, who wrote about the vagrant underworld in the 1980s and said that, 'The colourful eccentric tramp is a rarity. The vast majority of tramps are miserable wretches with personality and psychiatric disorders, or the plain unemployed and homeless'. Even some of the beggars themselves shared the view that begging was not what it used to be. Mayhew interviewed a man who had been a beggar for 70 years and his view of the world was that 'There is nothing like it nowadays. The new police and this b***** Mendicity Society has spoiled it all'.

There has always been a popular fear of the work-shy, who are seen as some sort of threat to those of us who live in houses and consider ourselves hard-working and respectable. George Orwell said, 'In childhood we have been taught that tramps are blackguards and consequently there exists in our mind a sort of ideal or typical tramp – a repulsive, rather dangerous creature who would rather die than work or wash and wants nothing but to beg, drink and rob hen houses'.

Today, although we have plenty of beggars, the press and public are more concerned with people who receive large sums in benefits and want nothing but to drink cheap lager and watch daytime television. Governments are still concerned about the danger posed by sturdy beggars and try to encourage a more productive way of life. Not for nothing is the dole or unemployment assistance called Jobseekers' Allowance.

Mayhew, a journalist who reflected the concerns and fears of his age, neatly summed up the relationship between the respectable and those who chose not to work:

There never was a time or place in which there were not to be found men anxious to avoid labour and yet to live in ease and enjoyment, and there never was a time in which other men were not, from their sympathy, their fears or their superstition, ready to assist the necessitous or those

who appeared to be so, and liable to be imposed upon or intimidated
according as the beggar is crafty or bold.

Some beggars ended their days in the most miserable circumstances.
After recounting how George Atkins Brine had been declared a second
Bampfylde Moore Carew, the editor of his biography goes on to say
that it would serve no good purpose to record any more of the life of
Brine, since from that time his life was simply the ordinary life of a
very ordinary beggar – he eventually retired from the road and spent
his declining years in Dorchester Workhouse.

However, there is always the possibility of redemption; people born
in the most difficult circumstances may have the initiative to escape
and make a success of themselves. W.H. Davies became a famous
poet; Mary Saxby became an evangelist and Bampfylde Moore Carew
may have won a lottery and been welcomed back into the fold by his
family.

For ten years, Henry Mayhew followed the career of a beggar boy,
whom he was able to recognize because he had an easily identifiable
squint. The boy's start in life was not good. At the age of four, he was
sent begging with his sister in pubs. Later, he sold flowers, matches
and song sheets and then he and his sister were dressed up in sailor
costumes and sent out to raise money by singing songs. The boy had
ambitions and tried becoming a boot-black, but this did not work
because the trade was controlled by organized groups. However, he
became a crossing sweeper in Endell Street, Covent Garden and
later had enough funds to set himself up as a costermonger selling
mackerel.

Although most colourful beggars have vanished from our streets,
any visitor to India will be taken back to the world we have lost. Real
and fake disabilities, people begging outside temples, street musicians,
children performing as acrobats at railway stations and even snake
charmers. Much of the literature about beggars – both that written by
beggars themselves, or by commentators such as Mayhew – stresses
the dishonesty behind much begging; sturdy rogues pretending to
have a terrible disease or disability or to be the victims of great misfortune. This air of disapproval continues to this day with notices in
London churches urging us not to give money to beggars.

However, it is impossible for us to tell whether an individual beggar
is a fraud or a deserving cause and it is always worth remembering the
advice given by Charles Lamb in his *Complaint of the decay of beggars in*

the Metropolis. He told the story of the bank clerk who for 20 years had walked from his home in Peckham and had dropped a halfpenny into the hat of a blind beggar in the Borough. When the beggar died, he left £500, then a small fortune, to the clerk. Lamb remarked 'Reader, do not be frightened at the hard words, imposition, imposture – give, and ask no questions. Cast thy bread upon the waters. Some have unawares (like this Bank clerk) entertained angels'. He advised that when a beggar approaches, do not try to save a small amount of money by disbelieving him, but treat him as a performer and pay your money to see a performance. After all, you have no way of knowing whether he is genuine or not.

Chapter Six

Conclusion

*If you are on this planet long enough,
you will become a direct or indirect
victim of one of these frauds*

While reading about sturdy beggars, con men and fraudsters, it is easy to become complacent, to think 'how could anybody be so foolish as to be taken in?' Why would an intelligent and sophisticated person fall for the Spanish Prisoner letter, or believe that a single document dealer such as Hofmann could find so many new and significant records? Surely nobody could be so crazy as to invest with Madoff? The truth is, of course, that many thousands of people over the years have been tricked and cheated and will continue to be until the end of time.

Many of the victims we have met were intelligent and sophisticated; Sir Frederic Madden, for example, was one of the leading manuscript scholars of his day and yet he believed that a signature in a copy of the works of Montaigne was genuinely Shakespeare's and, on the basis of this false assumption, built a fantastic castle in the air proving that the original spelling of the bard's name was Shakspere. Dickens and Elie Wiesel were nobody's fool, but both of them had the trick played on them.

Alex Dalmady, the man who revealed problems with Alan Stanford's empire, went even further. He said that 'if you are on this planet long enough then you will become a direct or indirect victim of one of these frauds. Sooner or later it will happen. It can be from being confident, trusting, naïve, greedy or careless. Or simply stupid. But it will happen'. This is because the greatest cheats have hit upon some great truths about human nature. Their insights are equally useful whether they are beggars telling a hard luck story, Nigerian scammers trying to persuade you that they have access to illegally acquired money or modern investment bankers running Ponzi schemes.

Bampfylde Moore Carew described some of these truths when he printed the dying speech of Clause Patch, King of the Beggars. He said that 'The two great passions of the human breast are vanity and pity; both of these have great power in men's actions, but the first the greater by far and he who can attract these the most successfully will gain the largest fortune'. Add greed and a sense of urgency to these two passions and we have a recipe for successful scamming.

Madoff understood the appeal to vanity, as did Tigg Montague; both men made it appear difficult to invest in their businesses and so attracted people who enjoyed the exclusivity that membership provided. Many forgers, such as the person who produced forgeries of rare American manuscripts, appealed to the vanity of collectors. The willingness of collectors to suspend critical judgement to acquire an item of great value was well-known in the eighteenth century, when there were jokes about antiquarians who had bought Falstaff's corkscrew. It was not just the victims who were vain.

Many tricksters took pride in their ability to put one over on their fellows and to demonstrate that they were cleverer than their victims. As a child, Mark Hofmann had enjoyed mystifying people with his magic and card tricks and got the same sort of thrill from his forgery. Some 300 years ago, Richard Bentley described the motives of forgers as either gain or 'glory and affectation as an exercise of style and ostentation of wit'.

Beggars and writers of begging letters appealed to people's sense of charity and even Mark Hofmann, the Mormon forger, was able to sell some of his fantasies to devout Mormons who wished to present them to the church. Equally, the great con men all relied on their victims' greed. The essence of a Ponzi scheme is that it offers returns way above what an ordinary investment would ever yield.

Where we see real genius in the scamming business is when people can bring two of these truths to bear at the same time and this was one of the strengths of both the Spanish Prisoner gang and some of their successors in Nigeria. They are able to appeal to people's greed (a hidden treasure) and their charity (a poor daughter locked up in a convent and desperate to return to family life). The other essential element in a good scam is to create a sense of urgency. This puts pressure on the victim and disorientates him or her. Go to buy a car; the salesman might tell you that he is able to offer you a special discount, but only if you agree to the deal on that day, because he needs to meet his monthly sales target. The Spanish Prisoner gang used similar techniques – there was an urgent need to rescue the daughter and recover the treasure. The beggars who feigned epilepsy or pretended to be drowning in the Serpentine were carrying this sense of urgency to an extreme.

Of course, any form of trickery, whether it is forged manuscripts, letters from a Spanish prisoner or a Ponzi scheme, does require a degree of credulity on the part of the victim. People are tricked because they are anxious to believe in the unbelievable – that somehow it is possible to beat the market, to find a valuable and rare manuscript, to stumble upon a hidden treasure. Tigg Montague appeared surprised but gratified at the number of people who would buy annuities or insurance policies, while knowing nothing about him or his company.

Part of the reason that the Spanish authorities did not pursue the Spanish Prisoner too vigorously was that they regarded his victims as credulous fools who had created their own downfall.

But it goes further than mere credulity; in the end, tricksters of all sorts rely on persuading their victims to believe things we know we should doubt. They persuade them that, in the words of the writer, Rick Grunder, 'they know something which we do not, that they have access to things that we could otherwise never hope to find'. Grunder was talking about Hofmann's forgeries, but he could equally well have been talking of the great Ponzi artists, who somehow persuaded their victims that they had access to secret financial information. Simon Worrall said that Hofmann was successful because he 'understood how flimsy the wall is between reality and illusion and how willing we are in our desire to believe in something, to embrace an illusion'.

To succeed, they need to persuade their victims that the hall of mirrors they have created is the real world. This requires remarkable skills; Henry Mayhew said that begging letter writers needed 'that shrewd perception of character peculiar to fortune tellers, horoscopists, cheap jacks and peddlars'. He could have equally been talking of beggars, fraudulent financiers or forgers.

Perhaps the most telling example of this use of shrewd perception of character comes from the 1897 letter from a man allegedly called Leopoldo Garcia of Valencia to Edgar Paul of Dorchester. It was a Spanish Prisoner letter, but it had some wonderful touches. Garcia urged Paul to be careful and to send the money back in a registered letter sealed with sealing wax. Once the money had been received, Garcia's wife and daughter would set off and he would send Paul a photograph of the daughter. They would travel to Maiden Newton Station and would carry a black handkerchief, so that he could locate them. The whole letter is a masterpiece of psychology, creating an air of mystery and excitement and luring Paul into a co-conspiracy with the gang. Inevitably Paul fell for it.

The most successful of the scammers were able to trap their victims into a world where reason and rationality were suspended. Thomas J. Wise had a remarkable talent for deluding his victims and ruthlessly exploited his friendship with John Henry Wrenn, who bought many of his forgeries. Wise was obviously hugely persuasive because after the finger of guilt had been pointed at him, his friends rallied round and the American bookseller Gabriel Wells printed a pamphlet defending him. Even more confused was the book keeper at a Berkley, Michigan law firm who, in 2002, stole $2.1 million from her employer and sent it to a 'Dr Mbuso Nelson' of Pretoria who had promised to pay her $4.5 million for helping transfer funds out of the country. Perhaps the most telling evidence of the total delusion of some victims was Norman Levy who, on his deathbed, told his children to trust Bernie Madoff.

Some of the cheats described in this book had a remarkable capacity to delude themselves. Although Hofmann produced a list of his forgeries, he has also confessed to forging documents that were in fact the work of other people. Like many other financial fraudsters, Madoff seems to have started his Ponzi scheme with a firm conviction that he would be able to recover from the financial hole he was in and return to being a legitimate businessman. Charles Ponzi was swept away with the success of his initial fraud and believed that he could eventually become a major force in US banking.

A few have, so far, not admitted to their faults; Allen Stanford is appealing against his conviction. The prize for the greatest piece of self-delusion goes to Bampfylde Moore Carew (or maybe to his editor). He makes a great play in his autobiography of his being elected King of the Beggars following the death of Clause Patch, the previous king. A great story and a great way to boost the sales of his book, but a total fantasy because Patch was a fictional character, having appeared in books a hundred years before Carew was born.

As well as great psychological skills, fraudsters need good practical ones. Acting skills were important to beggars, financial fraudsters and even to forgers who had to sell their products to potential customers. Rather more important were the skills needed to get good information about the people they were targeting. The fictional Clause Patch advised beggars to modify their techniques according to the type of person they were approaching. Mark Hofmann was able to use his knowledge of the Mormon Church to produce forgeries that he knew would be attractive to its elders. The Spanish Prisoner gang were particularly clever because in a number of cases they were able to persuade their victims that the prisoner and his poor daughter were somehow related to them.

However, not all our tricksters were very successful and we know about most of them because they finally got caught. A few forgers were not fully unmasked until after their deaths, while neither the Texas forger nor the man who forged the Himmler material were ever prosecuted. The most spectacularly successful of these tricksters was the Spanish Prisoner gang, which survived, largely unscathed for nearly 70 years. Some of the other cheats were remarkably unsuccessful, being caught within a short period. Two con men, Charles Ponzi and William '520 per cent' Miller lasted little more than a summer. The begging letter writer Alice Hammond was grossly incompetent. She used her maiden name and that of her daughter-in-law on begging letters and sometimes gave her real address in Bexleyheath. It did not require the skills of a Sherlock Holmes to catch Mrs Hammond and she spent frequent periods in prison. George Atkins Brine the nineteenth century 'King of the Beggars' also lacked the common sense needed to be a successful cheat and spent his life in and out of gaol as a result.

But, it has to be said, that on the whole the authorities have been remarkably unsuccessful in detecting and preventing the sort of crimes described here. Beggars are perhaps the exception to this and at different times the government has taken radically different approaches, ranging from extreme violence under Edward VI to the provision of night shelters and support services today. Even though their numbers have declined markedly there are still plenty of beggars on our streets.

Official attempts to curb other forms of activity have met with varying success. The Mendicity Society was remarkably good at identifying and prosecuting begging letter writers and the Nigerian government took the problem of scams so seriously that it included them as article 419 in their penal code. Few of the major forgers described here were caught as a result of official inquiries – most were identified by sharp eyed curators or collectors. Yet, Mark Hofmann, the greatest of them all, was not arrested for forgery but because he planted bombs which killed two people, while a third device exploded in his car seriously injuring him. His forging activities only came to light during subsequent police investigations.

As for the con men, Miller and Ponzi were imprisoned after some considerable delay by the authorities, but the greater tricksters Madoff and Sadleir were only caught because their schemes were collapsing under their own weight. Stanford was under investigation for years, but was only arrested after Alex Dalmady, a Venezuelan economist, published an article that demonstrated that his financial empire was built on very shaky ground. Those in the press and Parliament who believe that the answer is more and better regulation might well remember the words of Alex Dalmady, 'Scams will continue regardless of the regulatory hurdles thrown at them. They'll morph or mutate, much as pathological bacteria do when facing an antibiotic attack'.

Some of the crimes described in this book are solitary activities. In the sixteenth century, there was a belief that sturdy beggars were organized in gangs led by 'Upright Men'. Dickens's description of the gang in *Oliver Twist* was a contribution to this theme. Mayhew also gives some examples of organized teams of beggars, but both Mayhew and the people who wrote rogue literature enjoyed scaring their readers and the evidence from the surviving biographies of beggars is that they led solitary lives, coming together for a short time where necessary.

Begging letter writers too seem to have largely worked on their own, although there were some suggestions that they occasionally collaborated, swapping details of likely targets. Most of the forgers we have looked at were loners, conducting their mysterious craft in cellars or bedrooms, anxious to prevent anyone from discovering what they were doing. The possible exception to this rule may have been the Protocols of the Elders of Zion; their authorship is uncertain, but there was one suggestion that they were produced on the orders of the head of the Russian secret service in Paris.

Successful con men required a large infrastructure to raise money from their victims. Madoff ran a dishonest operation on a large scale for many years. His model was to rely on himself and a few close associates operating from a separate floor in a building that also housed the legitimate side of his business. Madoff sold his products through financial intermediaries and so his team was much smaller than Stanford's which sold direct to the public and had branches across the USA.

Although the Spanish Prisoner scam generated less money than the financial frauds, it lasted for much longer and was very complex. It was a huge business, involving the ability to conduct transactions in various languages. At its height, the gang was probably receiving the equivalent of £29 million a year in today's money and they had agents in Britain and possibly other countries as well. And as the scam lasted 70 years, two, if not three, generations were surely involved. It was pretty much a direct one-to-one sales business, identifying possible victims through post office directories, sending out personalized letters, negotiating with likely prospects, as well as maintaining agents within the Spanish Post Office and paying bribes where needed. This represents organized crime on an industrial scale in the pre-internet world and, in its structure, resources and longevity seems to have been the largest scam ever.

One interesting question is whether people have become less credulous over time. It is always tempting to believe that we are more sophisticated and aware than our ancestors. There is certainly some evidence pointing in that direction. Ponzi and William Miller offered laughably high rates of interest and it seems certain that only the most naïve people nowadays would not consider a return of 520 per cent a year as a scam.

Equally, the growing amount of information available online means that some scams today are not really sustainable. People who produced fake copies of rare printed documents, such as Foreman and Wise or the Texas forger, were successful because they were able to sell individual items to collectors for a high price. They had to be careful not to release too many examples that might push prices down or cause comment in the trade. In the modern era of eBay and specialist websites a sudden rise in the availability of rare documents would become quickly apparent and people would become suspicious.

However, the number of internet scams is growing every year and as people learn about one trick, the criminals move on to another one. In the end, it seems unlikely that human nature has changed over time and it is probable that cheats will always be able to make a good living. Alex Dalmady said, 'These rackets and hustles are as old as humanity itself and have been going on since Ug sold Og the "magic stone" that made fire'.

So, how can we avoid being scammed? The best way is to be aware of the methods which fraudsters use. If a financial organization is offering better returns than others, it may be questionable. It is manifestly unlikely that you will suddenly come into sudden wealth from an unknown source and anyone claiming that you are entitled to a fortune should be treated with caution. If someone is appealing to your generosity, particularly if it is for a cause you have never heard of, then be rightly suspicious. Scammers rely a lot on speed and a sense of urgency – you don't need to be in a hurry to hand over your money. Above all, remember Alex Dalmady's warning – it is inevitable that every one of us will fall victim to a fraud one day. What is important is not to put all your money in one place, even if the place you put it promises total safety and fabulous returns.

Don't put all your eggs in one basket and remember that if something is too good to be true, then it probably is. Sometimes the oldest advice is the best.

Appendix

Street Entertainers

Their standard fare seems to have been bawdy songs and they were closely associated with beggars and criminals

Street entertainers are part of a long tradition which has all but disappeared from our streets. In the past Britain's streets were much livelier places, yet nowadays they are largely devoid of entertainment. Only 50 years ago it was commonplace to hear the mellifluous hum of an accordion in the main thoroughfares of towns up and down the country. The accordion player would dangle a cloth bag for donations from his instrument and perhaps wore a notice round his neck, inscribed with the words 'BLIND Thank you'. Equally common was the staccato cheer of a barrel organ, complete with a tiny self-pitying monkey on a lead, and an elderly person bundled up on a chair turning the handle.

Today, as a result of strict policing, buskers play their violins, guitars and backing tapes in strictly designated spots and, in London, within the subterranean tunnels at underground stations. The lost world of street entertainment can be glimpsed in Edinburgh during the yearly festival or at Covent Garden in London, but has largely been lost in the town centres of Exeter, Manchester, Birmingham, Nottingham, Leeds, Bradford, and Glasgow.

However, as the following two vignettes of the street entertainers in the sixteenth and nineteenth centuries reveal, things were once very different. Let's take a look at a typical market day in Canterbury, in the sixteenth century. Mingling with the sounds from pens of sheep, pigs and cattle, the pedlars shouting their wares, piled up on trays hanging in front of them; the stench of manure, urine, putrefying vegetables and animal faeces underfoot; the clear and tuneful sound of voices can be heard, singing in harmony to the accompaniment of a fiddle, pipe and tabour. In the Tudor period street singers were known as minstrels and they performed at weddings, funerals and wakes, as well as in the streets. Their standard fare seems to have been bawdy songs and they were closely associated with beggars and criminals.

Within the crowd, the locals move aside to see a lumbering dancing brown bear. His minder brandishes a stick and holds the bear by a leash attached to his muzzle. A larger space is cleared for a group of six cavorting acrobats, ending with a human triangle, three standing on the shoulders of the others. Threading his way through the crowd is the town crier, clanging his bell and shouting the news of Drake's recent success against the Spanish Armada.

A crowd of yokels gathers round a juggler, or as we would now call him a street magician or conjurer. The Elizabethans commonly believed that jugglers had supernatural powers. We know a lot about sixteenth-century jugglers because a Kentish gentleman, Reginald Scot, was determined to stamp out this belief in the wizardry and power of jugglers. To achieve this he published his *Discoverie of Witchcraft* (1584), in which he explained how their tricks were performed. He was at pains to prove that witchcraft and magic were not real – witches could not contract with the devil, cast spells or fly in the air and the 'miraculous' displays by street magicians were simply the result of trickery to delude the audience.

In order to demonstrate this, Scot provided a remarkable catalogue of the various methods employed by jugglers. Some contemporary writers worried that street magicians might keep superstition alive among the credulous, who failed to see that they were simply prac-tising tricks and believed that they really did have supernatural powers. However, Scot argued that, 'if these things be doone for mirth and recreation and not to the hurt of our neighbour, nor to the abusing or prophaning of God's name, in mine opinion they are neither impious nor altogether unlawfull'. The most important thing was that the juggler should not claim divine powers and that, at the end of his performance, he should admit that it was all an act and not the result of supernatural activity.

In fact, although Scot had a serious purpose in writing his book, he still clearly loved to watch jugglers and provided a useful practical guide to emulating their tricks. If you want to know how to stick a bodkin through your head or put a ring through your cheek, then Scot's book will tell you how. Most of the acts he described are familiar today: pretending to move a ball from your hand to your mouth; palming coins; performing tricks involving boxes with false bottoms, etc. However, during the Tudor era most men carried knives and violence was never far from the surface. Some of the acts Scot described were a reflection of the age in which he lived – one trick appeared to involve thrusting a knife through the head of a chicken and then curing the chicken's wounds by use of magic words. In other cases he taught how people could cut off their noses. Sadly, my publisher forbade me to reveal these secrets in case of death or injury to my readers.

One trick I can reveal, which is probably Scot's most spectacular one, involved a juggler stabbing himself in the stomach, provoking shrieks of wonder and horror from the audience as blood spurted out of the wound. The secret to this trick involved creating a false stomach and chest out of cardboard, which could be attached to the front of the magician's body. Before putting it on he would fix a metal plate next to his skin and a bladder of sheep or calf's blood in front of the plate. He would attract a crowd in the street and offer to demonstrate his skill in return for money. He would stab himself with a dagger or bodkin and expand his stomach so the blood would spurt out. According to Scot, the essence of this trick is 'to use (with words, countenance, and gesture) such a grace, as may give a grace to the action, and moove admiration in the beholders'.

Once this trick went horribly wrong, as Scot described. A juggler performed the trick,

> *at a tavern in Cheapside from whence he presentlie went into Powle's churchyard (St Paul's) and died. Which misfortune fell upon him through his own follie as being then drunken and having forgotten his plate which he should have had for his defense.*

Some of the most intriguing tricks Scot mentions are not clearly described. These include a feat making it appear that a cat is dragging a person through a pond, or that a gaggle of geese are pulling a log, but he does note that this trick should be performed some way off from the audience. Equally, he refuses to explain exactly how to make it appear that wine is pouring out of your ears.

The Elizabethan juggler's great set piece was the beheading of John the Baptist. It was really a *tableau vivant*, where astonished spectators saw the legs and torso of John the Baptist sticking out from one end of a table, while his head rested on a pewter plate at the other. This effect was created by cutting two holes in a table. Two men hid under the table – one stood on his head, so that his torso and legs appeared from one hole, while the other put his head through a hole at the other end of the table, resting on a pewter dish. The picture was made more realistic because dough kneaded with bullock's blood was used to represent severed flesh. Doubtless people in the audience screamed and fainted.

Let us now enter a nineteenth century street scene, near one of London's famous rookeries, home to paupers, criminals and those on the verge of the criminal underworld. By this time *tableau vivant* displays had gone out of fashion. John the Baptist had been replaced by a music hall act involving sawing the woman in half. The streets look quite different, too. They have pavements with sturdy metal bollards to prevent carts and carriages running over the pedestrians, while horse-drawn carriages and omnibuses' wood and metal wheels scrape over the shiny cobbles. Horses whinny and an old nag takes a break with its face buried deep in a jute nosebag, while his driver unloads tea chests from the cart. A dirty faced urchin sweeps aside the piles of steaming brown horse manure, so that a lady in a red crinoline can cross the road without getting her skirt and shoes mucky. The air is still thick with pungent smells – chimney smoke, manure and stinking vegetables. The cry of the water-seller with buckets yoked across her shoulders, melds with the ringing bell of the pie man carrying a tray on his head and the light voice of a young girl with a large wicker basket calling 'Lavender, Sweet Lavender'.

The voices of street singers can be heard above the hubbub. They concentrate on hymns or popular songs of the day. In other streets nearby, social investigator Henry Mayhew has reported seeing a blind Scotch Violoncello player, a German band, a French hurdy-gurdy player, a Scotch piper and a dancing girl. Victorian singers did not share modern sensitivities and, in the middle of the century, there was a fashion for 'blackface' singers, (sometimes called Ethiopians) – who blackened their faces and sang what they believed were songs belonging to the black people from the United States. Mayhew interviewed a member of a six-man troupe of 'blackface' minstrels, who sang round Oxford Street and the various street markets of central London.

The tradition of street magicians also continued throughout the nineteenth century. Mayhew described the tricks they used, and many of these, involving coins or cards, were familiar from Scot's book. He also interviewed sword, knife and snake-swallowers, jesters, clowns and stilt walkers, ballet performers, tight rope dancers, strong men and owners of dancing dogs – all of whom would have been recognised by Scot. Nevertheless, some nineteenth century street performers exploited new technologies unavailable in Scot's day. For example, Mayhew spoke to a man who had a number of telescopes, which he set up on clear nights and charged people a penny a time to look at the stars. This seems to have been a lucrative business because he made about £125 a year from it in 1850 – equivalent to about £10,500 today. Unusually for a street entertainer, the telescope man also had a day job as a tailor and the telescopes were a sort of hobby for him.

Mayhew also spoke to an Italian whose father had been a poor farmer in Parma; he had come to London and made his living by exhibiting mechanical figures, which he had designed and had made in Germany. His great pride was an elephant, which moved its legs, tail and trunk, while the driver would lift his arm and the Indian aristocrat sitting in a howdah raises his bow and arrow. He also spoke to a peep show proprietor who worked the street markets. Unlike the erotic shows of the twentieth century, the mid-Victorian shows focused on reproductions of popular plays, historical events and, best of all, murders. Mayhew's peep show proprietor had created a show about the notorious 1849 murders at Stanfield Hall, in which a tenant farmer James Rush murdered his landlord and the landlord's son. He claimed this was even more lucrative than his recreation of the Battle of Waterloo.

By the 1930s, the aristocrats of the street entertainers were the acrobats who, according to George Orwell could earn £5 a week on a good pitch. Organ grinders earned between £2 and £3, but had to pay 15s rental for the organ. At the other end of the scale, pavement artists, who draw more-or-less skilful pictures in chalk have a long history. To some extent they too were the product of technological improvement, as they started out in business from the seventeenth century, when cities began to be equipped with smooth flat pavements. An 1829 drawing by George Cruikshank, the caricaturist and book illustrator, is one of the earliest published images of a pavement artist, or 'screever', as they were traditionally known, probably from the Latin word *scribere* meaning to write. The term screever was used in Walt Disney's film *Mary Poppins* in 1964, to describe Bert as a pavement artist.

Early screevers seem to have focussed on writing slogans, appeals for money or other phrases, often with elaborate borders, and then to have moved on to creating pictures. In Victorian times, a small group of screevers worked at night, their pictures illuminated by candles. From the 1880s, the introduction of bright street lamps on the Thames Embankment made it a haven for London's night artists. Sadly they seem to have vanished as a result of the blackout in the First World War.

The zenith of the street pavement artist appears to have been just before the First World War and the 1911 census contains a large number of people who describe themselves as 'Pavement Artist' or 'Street Pavement Artist'. Sadly the officials who compiled the statistics from the census did not distinguish between pavement artists and other types of painters and sculptors and consequently it is not possible to know for certain how many there were, though a contemporary London newspaper estimated there were 500 of them in the city.

The life of a pavement artist was a tough one, as they were dependent on the weather, as much as on the generosity of passers-by. George Orwell befriended a pavement artist called Bozo, who had a tragic life story. Bozo trained as a house-painter and went to Paris as a young man, where he had become engaged; sadly his fiancée was killed in an accident and Bozo became disabled as a result of a fall from scaffolding. He returned to London, where he made a living by drawing political cartoons. He could make £3 on a good weekend and averaged about £1 a week, but, although he did well in the summer, he was half-starved in the winter

Gradually during the twentieth century street entertainers disappeared from our streets into circuses and variety shows on the stage and television. Pavement artists have given way to illicit graffiti. However, as a throwback *tableau vivant* sprang back to life with a vengeance in the 1980s, possibly based on Gilbert and George's pioneering 'Singing Sculpture' of 1970. Now you can hardly walk down the Thames Embankment or through Trafalgar Square in London without seeing a horde of men and women covered in silver metallic powder standing on milk crates striking poses.

Bibliography

Chapter One: The Greatest Con Men

Dalmady, Alex, 'Duck Tales', Veneconomy (2004) (available at *www.scribd.com/mobile/doc/12923109*).

Dickens, Charles, *Little Dorrit* (1857).

Dickens, Charles, *Martin Chuzzlewit* (1844).

Dunn, Donald H., *Ponzi: The Incredible True Story of the King of Financial Cons* (2004).

Henriques, Diana B., *Bernie Madoff: the Wizard of Lies* (2011).

Kurdas, Chidem, *Political Sticky Wicket: the Untouchable Ponzi Scheme of Allen Stanford* (2012).

Markopolos, Harry, *No One Would Listen: a True Financial Thriller* (2011).

O'Shea, James, *Prince of Swindlers, John Sadleir MP, 1813–1856* (1999).

Sarna, David E.Y.; Malik, Andrew, *History of Greed: Financial Fraud from Tulip Mania to Bernie Madoff* (2010).

Chapter Two: Document Forgers

Baines, Paul, *The House of Forgery in Eighteenth-Century Britain* (1999).

Bott, Val; Wisdom, James, 'Lieut-Col Shipway's Pedigree', *Brentford and Chiswick Local History Journal*, No. 5 (1966).

Barker, Nicolas, 'Textual Forgery', in Mark Jones (ed.), *Fake, The Art of Deception* (1990).

Barker, Nicolas; Collins, John, *A Sequel to an Enquiry into the Nature of Certain Nineteenth Century Pamphlets by John Carter and Graham Pollard* (1983).

Dendy Bosanquet, Helen, *Social work in London, 1869 to 1912; a History of the Charity Organisation Society* (1914).

Bozeman, Pat (ed.), *Forged documents: proceedings of the 1989 Houston conference organized by the University of Houston Libraries* (1990).

Carter, John; Pollard, Graham, *An Enquiry into the Nature of Certain Nineteenth Century Pamphlets* (1934).

Cross, Nigel, *The Common Writer* (1988).

Fowler, Simon, 'Some of the Society's special collections', *Genealogists' Magazine*, 26:11 (2000).

Freeman, Arthur; Ing Freeman, Janet, *John Payne Collier: scholarship and forgery in the nineteenth century* (2004).

Groom, Nick, *The Forger's Shadow* (2002).

Houghton, Beth, 'Art libraries as a source of false provenance', *69th IFL General Conference and Council*, 2003 (available at *http://archive.ifla.org/IV/ifla69/papers/047e-Houghton.pdf*).

Landesman, Peter, 'A Twentieth Century Master Scam', *New York Times*, Online edition, 18 July, 1999 (available at *www.nytimes.com/1999/07/18/magazine/a-20th-century-master-scam.html*).

de Michelis, Cesare, *The Non-existent Manuscript: A Study of the Protocols of the Sages of Zion* (2004).

Rabinowicz, Oskar K., 'The Shapira Scroll: A Nineteenth-Century Forgery', *The Jewish Quarterly Review*, New Series, Vol. 56, No. 1 (July, 1965), pp. 1–21.

Schoenbaum, Samuel, *Shakespeare's Lives* (1991).

Schoenbaum, Samuel, *William Shakespeare, A Documentary Life* (1975).

Sillitoe, Linda; Roberts, Allen D., *Salamander: The Story of the Mormon Forgery Murders* (1988).

Taylor, Thomas W., *Texfake: An Account of the Theft and Forgery of Early Texas Printed Documents* (1991).

Thomas, David, 'Forgery in the Archives', *Archives* 34 (April, 2009), pp. 21–5.

Worrall, Simon, *The Poet and the Murderer: A True Story of Literary Crime and the Art of Forgery* (2002).

The files relating to the Himmler Forgeries are held at the National Archives under the reference RW 4. This includes the forgeries and copies of reports by forensic examiners and other papers, including correspondence with Dr Ernst Haiger, who originally unmasked the scam.

Publications relating to the Revels accounts include:

Law, Ernest, *Some Supposed Shakespeare Forgeries* (1911).

Stamp, A.E., *The Disputed Revels Accounts* (London, 1930).

Tannenbaum, S.A., *Shakespere* (sic) *Forgeries in the Revels Accounts* (1928).

Chapter Three: Begging Letter Writers

Dickens, Charles, 'The Begging Letter Writer', *Household Words*, Vol. I (1850), pp. 169–72.

Trow, M.J., *War Crimes, Underworld Britain in the Second World War* (Pen & Sword, 2008).

The careers of many begging letter writers can be traced through the criminal registers at The National Archives. Two research guides – *Looking for Records of a Criminal or Convict* and *Sources for Convicts and Prisoners* – are both available through The National Archives website (*www.nationalarchives.gov.uk*) and may help you understand the records.

There are some specific files on begging letters at The National Archives, particularly:

HO 45/9749/A58152 (which contains a list of nineteenth century cases taken by the Director of Public Prosecutions).

MEPO 3/1440 (Metropolitan Police, Office of the Commissioner, Correspondence and Papers, Special Series. FRAUD. Alice Hammond, persistent begging letter writer 1917–1940).

Nineteenth century newspapers contain many stories of begging letter writers. *The Times* Digital Archive is available online through your local library and the commercial British Newspaper Archives website contains millions of pages from local newspapers.

Chapter Four: The Spanish Prisoner

Cormac, Herley, *Why do Nigerian Scammers Say they are from Nigeria* (available at *http://research.microsoft.com/pubs/167719/whyfromnigeria.pdf*).

Griffiths, Arthur, *Spanish Prisons: the Inquisition at Home and Abroad, Prisons Past and Present* (1910).

Glickman, Harvey, 'The Nigerian "419" Advance Fee Scam: Prank or Peril', *Canadian Journal of African Studies*, Vol. 39 No. 3 (2005).

There is no standard published work on the Spanish Prisoner case. This chapter is based on extensive research at The National Archives and the Royal Mail Archive, in particular the following files:

The National Archives:
CO 323/641
HO 45/10022/A55279
MEPO 3/170
FO 227/8
FO 227/26
HO 144/21354
HO 45/10500/120541
HO 45/9606/A2527
MEPO 3/3050
FO 72/2228
The Royal Mail Archive:
POST 30/1877B

Chapter Five: Sturdy Beggars

Brine, George Atkins, *The King of the Beggars* (1883).

Dickens, Charles, 'Departed Beggars', *Household Words*, Vol. 5 (1852).

Dickens, Charles, *The Seven Poor Travellers* (1855).

Dickens, Charles, *The Uncommercial Traveller* (1860).

Davies, W.H., *The Autobiography of a Super-Tramp* (1908).

Davies, W.H., *Beggars* (1909).

Egan, Pierce, *Life in London or, the Day and Night Scenes of Jerry Hawthorn, esq., and his elegant friend, Corinthian Tom, accompanied by Bob Logic, the Oxonian, in their rambles and sprees through the Metropolis* (1821).

Hitchcock, Tim, *Down and Out in Eighteenth Century London* (2004).

Hughes, William R., *A week's tramp in Dickens Land* (1891).

Kinney, Arthur F., *Rogues, Vagabonds and Sturdy Beggars* (1990).

Lucy, William Henry, *Faces and Places* (1892).

Mayhew, Henry, *London Labour and the London Poor* (1851–1861).

McMullan, John L., *The Canting Crew: London's Criminal Underworld, 1550–1700* (1984).

Orwell, George, *Down and Out in Paris and London* (1933).

Roberts, M.J.D., 'Reshaping the Gift Relationship, the London Mendicity Society and the Suppression of Begging in England', *International Review of Social History*, XXXVI (1991), pp. 201–31.

Rose, Lionel, *Rogues and Vagabonds, Vagrant Underworld in Britain, 1815–1985* (1998).

Saxby, Mary, *Memoirs of a Female Vagrant* (1806).

Index